Made in the USA
Las Vegas, NV
26 January 2024

84813752R10129

DON'T LET THE TAIL WAG THE DOG

RONY ZAGURSKY

DON'T LET THE TAIL WAG THE DOG

The journey of
growing your company
without everything
depending on you

SAMEN
SERVICIOS EDITORIALES

DON'T LET THE TAIL WAG THE DOG
The journey of growing your company without everything depending on you

Edition and editorial design: SAMEN Editorial®
Cover: SAMEN Editorial®
Artwork Design: Adela Galante
Translator: Stephanie Kohab
Editorial consultant: Ken Emmond

First edition – 2020
D. R. © 2020, Rony Zagursky
Images pages (38, 44, 46, 90, 168, 178, 180) original whiteboard
"Designed by katemangostar / Freepik"
Graphic (page 68) intellectual property Adizes Institute

I.S.B.N. | 978-607-99875-0-3
I.S.B.N. eBook | 978-607-99875-1-0

All rights reserved. Partial or total reproduction of this book is not allowed, nor its incorporation to an informatic system, or its transmission in any way or through any medium, either electronic, mechanical, photocopied, recorded or others, without an expressed or written authorization from the author.

"Growing costs, and costs a lot". As Rony well mentions, starting a business is a long and sinuous road. Therefore we don't need to travel it alone. Books like this provide a wide vision of how to make fewer mistakes, how to do things in a different way and, naturally, when we have the privilege of having a good coach that guides us, he can help us avoid some mistakes and accompany us along this wonderful road. We will have better results, we won't feel so alone, and we will be able to create an "enterprise" to achieve our mission of "creating value" and making history.

Abraham (Avi) Bleier, Garabatos CEO
Mexico

Very inspiring, entertaining book that invites you to keep reading. Gives a simple way to switch the mental chip for transforming the enterprise and its leaders.

Helios Herrera, writer, lecturer, businessman,
creator of "Cámbiate el Chip" program
Mexico

If you want to scale your business and not feel trapped, you should read this book, which provides the guidelines to achieve that.

Dan Schwarzblat, founder and CEO of
Chilim Balam
Mexico

Definitely a book to share with my team and with other CEOs who wish to grow without sacrificing their Freedom.

Moisés Marcovich, founder and CIO of Grupo Sinestesia
(El Japonez, La Nonna, Buena Tierra and others)
Mexico

"Don't Let the Tail Wag the Dog is a powerful and instructive book for business leaders. Rony Zagursky hits the bullseye with his understanding of teams and how to solve the problems that suboptimize team performance. If you lead a team or develop leaders, read this book."

Mark E. Green
Author of Activators - A CEO's Guide to Clearer Thinking and Getting Things Done and Creating a Culture of Accountability; speaker, business and leadership growth coach to CEOs and executive teams
USA

So many leadership books are written that focus on growing your business or taking care of your employees. Rony has written an amazing book that focuses on taking care of yourself, your family, your business and your legacy.

Howard Shore, Best Selling Author, National Speaker,
and CEO of Activate Group, Inc.
USA

Rony is right on target with his understanding of teams and how to solve the problems that prevent teams from becoming effective.

Kevin Lawrence, author of Your oxygen mask first,
and advisor of CEOs and their directive teams
Canada

Amazing book. I recommend it for anyone leading a team or training leaders.

Alex Vorobieff, CEO Highmark Communications
USA

A book that seeks to inspire you through stories, information, statistics, tools, apps and events. It gives you a simple and applicable map of organizational change, to make the company a better workplace, more profitable and that allows it to grow.

Wolf Bielas, CEO Wolfpack Ventures
USA

A book that marks a map of change and organizational development. A must-read for anyone feeling trapped and wanting to develop their business.

Ferenz Feher T., CEO Feher Consulting
Mexico

Many times, in daily operation we get lost in the details and don't follow the original strategy. This book makes you aware of it and allows you to consolidate the strategy, while adding details of tuning. Rony addresses these topics in a clear and operational way.

Alberto Modiano, VP Supply Chain
Nestlé Mexico

Rony is a great coach who cares for his clients and has made tremendous difference in their professional and personal lives. This book will allow all of us to get a glimpse of what he is capable of. Well worth reading for anyone.

Abhay Sisodiya, strategist and international business coach.
Partner of Maher Advantage Inc.
Canada

Recommended and required reading for every businessman. Rony uses a fictitious but very real story as a teaching method, which makes it easy to comprehend. The author allows us to enter Dan's mind and feel how difficult it is to look in the mirror, accepting that maybe in some cases the tail is wagging the dog.

Dany Shor, CEO and founder of Pygsa Advertising SA de CV,
Pide un access SA de CV and Taimingo SA de CV
Mexico

The reality is that on many occasions there is a lack of strategy and consequent execution to carry out these changes. Changes require new behaviors from people, and it is a very difficult thing to achieve. Each one in their position lives in a "comfort zone", even though they complain about it. Changes are frightening and because of that there is so much failure in business. In this book Rony explains to us with a crushing truthfulness, how to visualize this problem and give it a solution.

Lluís M. Gras Balaguer, business educator, Scale Up business,
author of the book *El Pegamento de las Organizaciones*
Spain

Having known Rony for a decade, I can vouch for the journey that has led him to be a credible author delivering valuable content and tools to business owners. Rony's book is based on his own journey, and the experience of helping entrepreneurs build great businesses. It contains practical tools to use regardless of what comes at you as a growth business leader. The narrative approach, along with the storytelling connects the head and heart of the reader, often addressing the most challenging areas that business leaders are fearful to deal with: the loneliness of leadership, the consistent stress from growth needs; but also the joy of success and accomplishment!

Keith Cupp, founder and CEO Gravitas Impact Premium Coaches
USA

Strategy, vision and innovation on how you can reduce your workload while increasing your profits, delivered through an exciting and engaging fable. This remarkable book, *Don't let the tail wag the dog,* will give you the insight needed to identify and deal with toxic clients, employees and suppliers, while creating a systemized business that can efficiently run without you.

Cindy Ashton, Award-Winning TV Host of #CindyUncorked,
Singer/Entertainer, Keynote Speaker & Presentation Trainer
USA

Entrepreneurs are like emperors, always looking for new territories to add to their empire; however, it is this expansion fueled by explosive success that often ends up by weakening the foundations of their endeavor. That is the point from where Rony Zagursky departs, to take us through a story that is a must-read for those who dream of scaling their businesses.

Felipe Del Rio, business strategy coach
Peru

Rony uses a story as a training method, which makes a very easy and understanding reading. Recommended for all CEOs and their teams.

Cloe Madanes, President, Robbins-Madanes Training
USA

TABLE OF CONTENTS

"Even in moments when you are stuck in the sand, someone comes out to help you."

Let it go and trust.

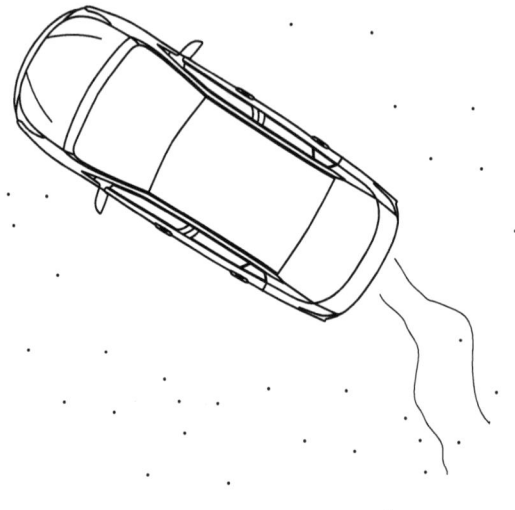
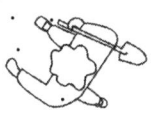

ACKNOWLEDGEMENTS

Thanks!

Writing a book is more difficult than I thought and more rewarding that I could have ever imagined.

Adela, none of this would have been possible without your support and trust in me: all those days of debates, reviewing drafts, making spaces to land my ideas on paper, post its, many books everywhere, many hours of confinement and nights of no sleep … above all, believing that I can inspire possibilities and make a real impact in people's lives. You chose to share your life with me and every day you teach me something new, primarily: "to let go and trust".

I would like to thank the people who have helped me throughout my life.

To my family, that has always supported me in my adventures.

To my mom, for teaching me the importance of dedication and strength that carried her five children forward.

To Pepe, for listening to me in critical moments that required my decision.

To Olga, for always being supportive and a pillar in my life; there were countless nights when we stayed awake all night talking in the kitchen.

Dany, for being someone who gives me a new perspective of things.

Roxy, for your tenacity, patience and dedication.

To my nephews, who all have been a fountain of knowledge in many ways: with each one of you I learn something and love to see how you develop different personalities and paths.

To my brothers, sisters and mother-in-law who have been a support fountain of creativity and perspective that makes me be more creative and adds value to our environment.

To my friends, who have been a fountain of joy, perspective and adventures. Wherever I have lived, I have counted on a community of friends that have

been for me through thick and thin, that have brought me a shoulder when I wanted to cry and a lejaim when I wanted to celebrate.

I extend my gratitude and respect to amazing people who have guided me along my way, whom I consider teachers: David Chávez, Moiseés Marcovich, Alberto Modiano, Alejandro Romo, Jim Tenuto, Mark Green, Paul O'Kelly, Alnoor Kassam; Coach in a Box team; Korn Ferry team; Gazelles team; Gravitas team; Frost and Sullivan team, Executive Forums, Diana Neuner, Jacob Szmuilowicz, Howard Shore, Kevin Lawrence, Alex Vorobieff, Travis Medley, Peter Boolkah, Ed Capaldi, Keith Cupp, Ricardo Chávez, Óscar Bonfil, Abhay Sisodiya, Helen Attridge, Eliezer Davidsohn, Chicole Ghitis, Aquiles Núñez, Helen Valleau, Jamie MacRae, Dorothy Holden, Doris Vega, Heydi Abreu, Sergio Montes de Oca, Claude Strickner, Carlos Sclar.

To the Habonim Dror community, that was a school of life, where I learned the art of non-formal education, the sense of belonging and collaboration.

Adela Mez, thank you for your support with the amazing pictures that were used for publishing this book.

Also, I would like to thank all of those leaders of thought that have influenced and changed my way of thinking; who I have the privilege of knowing and from whom I have directly learned: Verne Harnish, Patrick Lencioni, Anthony Robbins, Cloe Madanes, Brad Smart, Dan Ariely, Ryan Holiday, Tim Ferris, John Warrillow, Daniel Pink, Salim Ismail, Tony Hsieh, Kevin Lawrence, Howard Shore, Mark Green.

To all my clients who have challenged my way of thinking and trusted me, and also all those CEOs and directive teams who have given me the honor of being coach, facilitator, and allowing me to assist them in their processes of organizational growth. Furthermore, you have allowed me to obtain more knowledge and experience; you challenged me to be the best version of myself and have the best tools to confront greater challenges that were presented.

I consider myself lucky to have met you and to have traveled part of our adventure with you in this giant rock that travels through space.

INTRODUCTION

Growth leads to complexity and complexity is an organizational cancer that can kill companies slowly if not handled correctly. Therefore, we can understand why only a few companies manage to overcome the Start-up stage to become a company that lasts beyond the existence of the owner. While the company grows, it requires more attention from the founder. This implies a sacrifice of time, freedom and money, which the owner intended to have more of when starting a company, not less. This is because, when a company grows, it starts to implement lots of temporary solutions that eventually become permanent, and later turn into habits that finally become laws. But these temporary solutions were not necessarily the right ones for the long-term progress of the company. These solutions were probably good at the time they were needed, and also useful. But as time passed, they stayed permanently and silently without anyone remembering that these decisions changed the rules of the game and the way of operating, creating complexity, which is what silently kills an organization. Those solutions will eventually become habits that we repeat without noticing; they turn into a regular part of our lives.

It is like the story of a dolphin in the middle of the sea. The tuna happily greets its dolphin friend and asks him: "How's the water temperature today?", to which the dolphin answers: "What is water?". This means that the dolphin is so immersed in that reality that it cannot even distinguish that it is surrounded by water.

Something similar happens to the owner of a growing company: they live with a series of discomforts, frustrations and complexities that are created by themselves and are so evident but hidden for their own eyes, just like water for this dolphin. It is difficult to identify what doesn't work when you are the one immersed in that reality.

CEOs who founded their companies have the courage, luck or madness to start a business, facing on a daily basis the challenges that lead not only to growing the company, but also the challenges of surviving every day, feeling distressed by not having the money necessary to meet the next payroll, clients' dissatisfaction, competitors' threats, operative inefficiency, staff turnover; frustration for not having a team that understands their ideas, plans and vision, absence of a team you can delegate tasks to; complaints from their wife, mainly for not being present with their family. It is as if that dream of freedom transformed into a daily routine of distress for finishing the day without having control over the company. It seems like the tail is wagging the dog, and not the other way around.

It is the CEO/founder who is at the mercy of the company's needs, feeling trapped in a vicious circle of urges, complaints and frustrations. It all depends on him, frustrated and trapped.

At the very bottom, there is a problem of lack of confidence and working method. Centralized decisions and controls prove that the CEO doesn't have the right people around him, people whom he trusts completely, who won't steal or make mistakes; for example, the CEO thinks he needs to be the one who executes banking operations because he doesn't trust his team.

Apart from that, the lack of a work methodology and / or system means that everyone does things as they think they understand them, for which, unfortunately, they don't have the complete perspective or the experience of the CEO. That's why they make many mistakes, which are not permitted; on the contrary, they are punished. The leader of the organization wants things done as he would have done them, so instead of delegating, he paralyzes. Many problems start in the head of the organization, with the CEO, and this gives us a huge advantage, because change is under internal control.

This is a very common situation, there are many CEOs/Founders around the world that live with frustration, lack of control and solitude while leading a company and a family by themselves, hiding many of his thoughts. This creates the need to pretend, before family, friends, society, company and even with the competition, that everything is under control,

but underneath, they have the feeling of being impostors, knowing things aren't working correctly.

Nevertheless, there are different ways of doing things. These precise ways of doing things differently allows them to take back control of their company, not only to live a happy present with abundance, good results and reputation, but also to secure the future of the company as a legacy and prosperity for the family.

There is a high level of dependency on the founder by the company, for which he can't be absent for even seven days to go on vacation with his family without having to take the token or bank passwords, without fearing that things may go down the drain at any moment; feeling that dependency because many decisions pass through his hands every day. So it is very important to have the mobile or computer nearby, even if he is trying to enjoy the sand castle that he is building with his children. This could lead us conclude that the founder doesn't have a business, but rather a self-employment, with a very high level of responsibility, and a potential of great benefits.

This is the reality in which many CEOs/founders live, but is not the reality they should expect. There are different ways of doing things; the problem is that they don't know it, and that is normal because we live in a world where everyone pretends things are good, and all the support and attention is for start-up companies or corporates.

Mid-sized companies, fast-growing companies, better known as Scale-ups, have predictable behaviors of which some are adequate and others are toxic. In this book, we will tackle some of the toxic behaviors and solutions to correct the company's direction and execution.

Reality may be very different for founders/CEOs if they have a company where NOT everything depends on them, in which he can be absent knowing everything will still work correctly; where he can have better control, where he is the leader who moves the company, as a dog does with its tail, and not the other way around.

Likewise, if you or your company doesn't live this reality of stress and frustration yet, this book will be of great help in implementing

methodologies and tools, assuring healthy growth and avoiding many common growth traps.

The process of change is as painful as setting a broken bone, which people say hurts more than when it broke, but it's worthwhile because the benefits are huge. Among these will be the possibility of focusing on activities that he enjoys doing and adding value, catching up on sleep and not taking sleeping pills; being close to his family, getting results, profit, cash in the bank, a trustworthy team and a strategic plan which can go beyond the founder's life, making it possible to leave a legacy. Therefore, this book is a guide with the first steps that you have to take so you can grow your company in a healthy way.

We can't solve a problem at the same level that we created it. Thus, we should learn about the next "level." As time goes by, we learn more and more, and realize that the decisions we made in the past weren't the best ones. Today we know that, but the reality is that back then, when we made them, they were right.

Knowing more will help you identify things in a better way. Therefore, this book will be a path through a fictitious story based on the compilation of real situations that have occurred to me with countless clients throughout my career: Dan is the leader of his company, Plastypack, and wants to take control over it. He wants it to grow, but not at the cost of his health, well-being and family. So, Dan and the reader's level of consciousness evolve to apply changes.

Let's turn this distress into an adventure, identifying what is not working and putting into action good practices that have been used in fast growing companies in different industries and countries. This will be a journey through Dan's experience to diagnose or identify toxic behaviors in the organization, generate solutions and more constructive habits.

Throughout the book, we talk about sums of money, for which I will use US dollars for practical reasons, since the book and tools are used internationally. At this moment the exchange rate is $22 MXN per dollar; $3,657 Colombian pesos per dollar; $0.8611 euros per dollar.

You will be exposed to a work methodology that helps companies develop and grow. The advantage of repeatable methodologies, is that they

can be measured and proven; they are a group of tested tools that carry a sequence of execution and when put to practice, help achieve the desired result. It's like having a dessert recipe; if you follow the steps correctly, you can obtain the same or similar result you obtained previously; and other people can follow the recipe and obtain the same result. This will make a happier journey and the decision making simpler.

I wrote this book precisely for this reason. I have been assisting and coaching corporate-sized companies for more than twenty years, as well as medium-sized companies, but above all, the development of the organizations and their leaders, of Scale Up companies, in eleven countries (Mexico, USA, Switzerland, Dominican Republic, Jamaica, Trinidad and Tobago, Cuba, Colombia, Nicaragua, UK, Israel).

For that, I have studied endless organizational development methodologies, finding great tools that work in each one of them which allow companies to obtain the best from each one.

How have I done it? By being a certified coach from Gazelles Lominger from Korn Ferry, Robbins Madanes Institute, Global Novations, DBM, Frost and Sullivan, ACN, Coach in a Box, as well as consulting many books and taking courses along my way, like in particular, Adizes. Above all, I have done it by putting into practice, over and over again, diverse tools in companies with radically different cultures, and also with products and services, each one different from the other, but in all of them I have identified that no matter the industry or the country of origin, the behavior of companies is predictable.

I have worked with clients from all types of industries in their process of change. I am an expert in the process of change and organizational growth. For example, without being an expert in food production, insurance sales, artificial intelligence, security boxes manufacturing, construction, data centers, marketing agencies and many others, I have confirmed that these tools work, like antibiotics work with people no matter their race, religion or nationality: they work because the human body is predictable and changeable, handled in a standard way. The same happens with companies.

I believe in the power of learning throughout the game; therefore, the transformation of the companies that I assist is through "non-formal education": I use frontal training, lectures, board games, books and more, to transform the members of the organization.

This book is written like a fable of a company's change and transition; the company is Plastypack, and Dan, the CEO. The goal is to help CEOs and their directive teams understand the reality they live in and get tools of change.

I write this book from the knowledge and truth that I uphold today. If in the future I realize or learn that the practices I use today aren't valid anymore, I will make a correction. As well, in order to keep things simple we will refer to Ceo's and founders, with the pronoun he.

My clients expect an honest and direct truth from me; they prefer knowledge over comfort, which makes our relationship special, because they hope to hear from me and my work team what they need to hear and not what they expect.

My job with the companies is to show the CEOs and their directive teams what is not working well, for the purpose of correcting it. I also applaud their victories, but they hired me not only to be their "cheerleader", but also their "devil's advocate".

If you are willing to hear what you need to hear, want to take control over the company, make the effort to change bad habits or toxic activities that are practiced at your company step by step, then this book will help you. I will draw you a path to a company with a controlled and happy growth, where the most difficult part is not implementing tools, but making them last through time, so they can become habits.

Some years ago, I was in a meeting with Dina Dwyer-Owens, who transformed the company she inherited from her father; she said a very true thing that has made an impact on the way I see and teach things to my clients: "Design what you want or deal with what you get".

It is fortunate that we can decide how we want the company to operate. We are not victims of the circumstances; we can choose and transform organizations. Everything depends on our decisions, on the tools that help us make better decisions that become more adequate habits.

Here you will find the initial information to increase your level of consciousness and make the dog wag the tail, and not the other way around.

In our webpage https://adaptable.com.mx/ and http://www.colanomue

vaalperro.com/ you can download free tools, formats, meeting agendas and more, so you can start implementing changes.

MAPPING THE REALITY OF THE COMPANY.

> ❱ A patient tells his doctor that his entire body is aching, that each time he touches some part with his right index finger it hurts. The Dr. examines him and tells him that the problem is not the body, but that his finger is broken.
>
> ❱ Companies try to fix everything at the same time, as if everything were a priority; nevertheless, it is important to find the root cause, to be able to identify and change the toxic habits. The most common one is the high level of dependency on the CEO/owner in the daily execution of the company.

Dan's secretary led me to his office and offered me something to drink. Dan will be arriving in ten minutes.

Rony: A peppermint tea would be perfect for me. Thank you.

I could see that Dan's desk was full of papers, bank tokens everywhere, some business books in the back, product samples, post-its with ideas, distributed on two walls, what seemed to be a list of things to do; in general, chaos. And then Dan arrived.

Dan: I apologize for the delay, I had to solve a daily operation emergency again, but now we are back on track.

Rony: Don't worry, the important thing is that now we are here. So, Samuel recommended me, great guy, I care and like him. I would like to know what he told you about me and why he thinks I can help you.

Dan: I like that, straight to the point.

Rony: Time is money.

Dan: A month ago I went to a finance training session with some other company owners. At lunch time I sat with Samuel, and while we were talking, I told him that I feel frustrated and trapped in my business, that everything depends on me, I feel my staff is not committed or doesn't have the right level of training; that I can't sleep at night, that I'm having troubles with my wife because of my stress and dedication to my business. That my dream of being a great entrepreneur and having freedom, financial independence and time, was just a fantasy. Almost immediately, he asked me if someone was helping me navigate the company, a coach or consultant, someone to help me put my ideas in order, to give me an external perspective and help me make more adequate decisions, to which I responded, I had no one like that. That's when he suggested I call you. He told me he was going through something similar and that now he is in a better professional and personal situation, so that's why I called you.

Rony: I'm glad Samuel is grateful and satisfied with my work enough to recommend my services. I would like to know a little more about your situation, to see if I really am a good solution for your needs, so I'm going to ask lots of questions. In advance, I offer you an apology, because you might feel uncomfortable with some of them, but I would like you to know that all the information you can provide me will give me more clarity on how to help you, so I ask for your total honesty and vulnerability.

Dan: I would like to think that I'll answer the questions with total honesty and try not to feel uncomfortable.

Rony: Before I start, I should tell you that at these meetings it is very common that CEOs try to "sell" me the great company that they have, because they are used to bragging about the success they have achieved. For me, that is not necessary; I need to know what is working and what is not working. We need to explore both sides of the coin so we can take control of the company and allow it to grow.

Dan: That's why I brought you here, to talk about what is not working correctly, but if at any time you feel that I'm "selling you" the company please let me know.

Rony: Also, I can assure you of the confidentiality of our conversation. A key part of my work is to have confidential information that weakens companies, because I work in those areas in particular. My success is your success. Tell me a little about the story of the company and where you're standing today.

Dan: It all started with the dream of becoming independent, of leaving the job that I had because it was drowning me. I didn't like to report or have a specific schedule, but, above all, it was the dream of having freedom, financially and of time, to be able to travel with my family and give them everything; by being an employee, my potential was limited. It was February 8th 2010, when I was talking to my friend Isaac, and he told me that he had problems with one of his suppliers and he couldn't find anyone who satisfied his packaging needs. Besides, that supplier was having financial problems, which meant his company was at risk. I had some capital and a great desire to start my own company, so I decided to ask him if I could buy his supplier. He could ensure the product purchase for the next couple of years; and he answered, "For sure, I really need to solve this problem, and what better way to solve it than together with you". So, I called Manuel, the owner of the company Plastypack, and a couple days later we met at his office. I told him I was interested in starting a new company and that I heard his company was having cash flow and customer satisfaction issues. To my surprise, Manuel told me that he felt old and tired, already had built his legacy so he need to continue living under this pressure, that he was willing to sell the company. He didn't want to lead it anymore or live every day feeling stressed. I asked him how much capital was needed to execute the company monthly. He told me that $68,000 USD were required per month. That amount of money covered the expenses, and the profit would be 16%, with an annual revenue of $954,000 USD per year. He told me he wanted $363,636 USD for the company. At the time, I had $45,000 USD saved. There was no way I could pay Manuel and keep supporting my family for the following months. So, we made an arrangement: that I would pay $410,000 USD over 3 years. I quit my job and, from that day on, the company was "mine." I went from being an

employee to the proud owner of Plastypack. I asked my friends, family, and other people I knew to lend me money for the initial payments so I could start running the company. It took time for employees to accept me as the new owner of the company. Some clients were very loyal to Manuel and were unwilling to work with me. But in the end, everyone understood that there would be a positive change to come, that we would be more efficient, and our clients would be happier. At the beginning, things were going well, we started to improve the operation, results and deliveries.

Rony: Ok, and now, if I'm here, it means that something is not working as it should, right? Tell me one thing that keeps you up at night.

Dan: Wow, only one? To be honest, there are many things keeping me up at night. The payroll, constant complaints from the customers, feeling trapped at a company which I don't feel prepared to handle, sales are going down. I feel exhausted because everything depends on me.

Rony: Which one of these nagging worries has the most impact on you?

Dan: I don't know. All of them.

Rony: I understand. Now, let me go deeper to see more clearly which one is the real source.

Rony: How many employees do you have working at the company?

Dan: 85.

Rony: What's your annual revenue and your profit?

Dan: $3,181,000 USD with 12% profit.

Rony: That 12% profit. Is that normal in your industry?

Dan: No, from what I know my strongest competitor has at least 20% profit.

Rony: From what we have at the moment, I can say that you have an execution problem. On one hand, you have a low profit regarding your industry, which puts you in a medium-term risk; and your efficiency is also very low, because your revenue per employee (RPE) is extremely

low. In Latin America, RPE is $50,000 USD of income per employee; in first World countries RPE is $100,000 USD of income per employee. As you can see, in your case we have $3,181,000 USD/85 employees, which gives us $37k USD; this shows us that you have more people than you need or that you should increase your sales without increasing your payroll.

Dan: I had never heard about that business indicator, but it correctly shows the status of the company.

Rony: In fact, it will be the indicator that we would use the most. It will give us clarity of the company's situation and will help you make better decisions. How accurately do you achieve goals set per quarter?

Dan: To be honest, I don't set goals for every quarter. In some way, I set goals for every month.

Rony: Ok. How many of those goals do you achieve?

Dan: I have never measured that, but I would say that I achieve 70%.

Rony: For the next question let me clarify a concept for you. Business directors are not necessarily linked to a "nobility title" or to salary; directors are those who lead a specific department. Typically, there is the director of Sales, Administration, Operations and Human Resources. Do you have a directive team to which you can delegate tasks and with whom you frequently get together to discuss strategy and progress?

Dan: Not exactly, I only have 2 directors, one for Sales and one for Operations, but they don't get along so I can't have meetings together with them, so I meet them separately.

Rony: So, you are like their messenger?

Dan: You could say that. I never thought of it like that, but you are right, I am like a messenger between them, which frustrates me a lot, because each one gives me a different version and I end up in the middle. For Administration and Human Resources, I have two other people, who are not at the same level as the first two, which makes it even more complicated.

Rony: Ok, let me understand this. So, instead of having a meeting with five people, you have five meetings, each with one person?

Dan: From that perspective, I think I have 15 meetings or more, each with one member, because I have to come and go with the information. You don't know how frustrating it is to feel that I am the one who's working for them and has to make all the decisions.

Rony: But that's exactly what you're doing. You do work for them. That's because you have the wrong work methodology. This situation is very common. Would you happily rehire the team that you have now?

Dan: Oh, that's a hard one, let me think about it. Mmn, actually no. There are many people I'm not happy with their performance or don't trust, but I don't have any choice, I need them at the company.

Rony: Maybe, the main reason you have an excess of people and drama at the organization is because you have people whom you don't trust or who have poor performance.

Dan: Yes, probably.

Rony: Besides, those who perform poorly and are still working at the company are a burden and / or obstacle, and even a bad example for the others.

Dan: Yes, definitely, but as I mentioned before, I need their help for the daily operation. As we are today, we cannot cope, I don't want to imagine if one of them leaves the company.

Rony: I understand your concern, but part of your inefficiency problem is because of those people. Change is painful and takes risks, so we are not going to change things wildly, but we are going to make painful decisions. How many days can you be absent from the company? And before you answer, let me clarify: by absence I mean being on vacation or in a course or maybe visiting suppliers in Germany or at a meeting with an important client in Colombia, so you don't have contact by email or by mobile, and you didn't bring tokens or bank passwords for making payments. Absence is zero presence in the day-to-day execution of the company. How many days can you be absent?

Dan: Oh, that question is really difficult and uncomfortable. To be honest, every time I'm boarding a plane, I feel that the world is going down the pipe while I'm on the plane. Realistically, I can be absent for

two days, as long as it is not payday, because if it is, there is no way I can be absent.

Rony: When your staff goes on vacation, are they absent? For how long do they go?

Dan: For me, it is very important that my staff can go on vacations and disconnect completely from the company, so that they recharge batteries. Time's up to them, but it's ideal if they can go for an entire week.

Rony: Do you get the irony in what you are saying?

Dan: Ouch, that question was really uncomfortable. It's true, they can be absent and I can't. But I don't know how I can change that.

Rony: That's why we're here. Right now, I'm only trying to understand your reality and find a way to help you. In case of an economic eventuality that prevents getting money into the bank account, a situation like H1N1 in 2009 or covid-19 in 2020, how many months or days could the company survive without the cash flow that you have now?

Dan: For that, I would need to call Alex, who is in charge of the administration and finances of the company. I'm going to text him and ask him to come over.

Rony: Ok, I'll wait. However, I think the answer would be "I don't know".

Dan: Exactly, I don't know how long, but my instinct tells me we could have cash flow for a month, which will give us enough gas in the tank to bear that time without having regular incomes.

Meanwhile, Alex enters the office with many papers on hand, and with a concerned look on his face.

Dan: Alex, let me introduce you to Rony, our business coach / consultant. He will help us change some things and make the company perform better. I wanted to ask you, in the hypothetical case that we didn't have money coming into our bank account, for any reason, but want to still operate normally, how long would our cash flow last?

Alex: I would say 15 days.

Dan: What? Only 15 days? I thought that we had enough reserves for a month.

Alex: No, that is why every payday I struggle to find the resources. We have problems with accounts receivable; there are many customers that miss their payment deadlines; the investment in new machines is having important repercussions; and the bank still hasn't increased the credit line.

I began to see how Dan was getting furious. Then he took a breath and told Alex that that was all, that he could go.

Dan: To make things worse, I don't know really where I stand; my staff won't tell me things as they are.

Rony: They don't tell you or you don't ask the right questions?

Dan: They don't tell me; my office is always open.

Rony: I would say both. They might not be telling you because they don't have enough trust in you, or they fear you?

Dan: I hope it's not because of fear, but I see your point. It may be possible that they fear telling me bad news. Each time I have less patience when they bring me problems instead of solutions.

Rony: In respect to "not asking the right questions"?

Dan: Well, I'm discovering that maybe I'm not asking the right questions. I have never asked Alex to tell me how much cash flow and reserve we have converted in days, and I think it's a very interesting number to review.

Rony: Not only interesting, it's vital to ensure the continuity of the company. In the ideal world, you should have six months of cash flow to face eventualities, because with that amount of money, you will feel much safer making decisions, above all, risky ones.

Dan: Six months? That's a lot of money.

Rony: Right, but how would you feel if you had that amount available?

Dan: Calmer, less stressed. It would be amazing, but I can't imagine how to make that happen at my company.

Rony: Well, that's something that may grow little by little. For example, we already know that your cash flow would last 15 days. A reachable goal for Alex and the organization would be to increase it to 17 days; once we achieve that, we set a new goal for 19 days. And so on, step by step you will be able to make it. It took you years to get to where you are now. Correcting the direction will take some time; it takes patience, clear vision, a team to work with and make them accountable.

Dan: I can see more clearly where our problems could be.

Rony: Good! because if we can't identify the root cause, it is impossible to have a solution that works in the long term. I just remembered a story, one of those told at the MBAs: it was about the owner of a factory who called a technician because he needed to fix his main machine. Some other technicians had gone to the factory, charged him a lot of money, and didn't fix the problem. This new technician didn't look like the best. They explained the problem. He took a stethoscope, asked them to start the machine and he began to listen carefully to the noises it made. After a few minutes, he asked them to stop the machine, took out a screwdriver and tightened one screw. Again, they started the machine, and it began working correctly. The owner asked the technician how much he owed him; the technician said: "$1,000 USD." "Wow, $1,000 USD for tightening a screw?" said the owner. The technician said: "No, $2 USD for tightening the screw, but $998 USD for knowing which screw to tighten".

Dan: I see, so, you are finding which screws to tighten?

Rony: Right. There's no point in trying to fix lots of things at the same time because that won't be effective. Handling too many priorities at the same time only leads us to do half of those things and not achieve any clear result. What are the three indicators of a company's success?

Dan: Sales, profit, and market share.

Rony: Those are definitions of company evaluation from the 80s and 90s that remain marked in the minds of CEOs. And I think they are insufficient, because they only show part of the big picture. **The three indicators with which we develop companies are: RPE (revenue per**

employee), Independence, which is the leader's absence in days, and last, reliability, which means, the percentage of fulfilled objectives.

Rony: **RPE,** the revenue per employee, is an index of efficiency used to determine the income generated per person who works at the company. The income index per employee is important for a company to determine the efficiency and productivity of the average employee. For many companies, their highest expenses are salaries and the benefits they give to employees. Therefore, companies mainly want a high RPE to compensate for the money paid to employees. Generally, a higher RPE indicates that the company is more productive and efficient. An index of revenue per employee is mainly used to analyze companies from service industries; however, it correctly highlights the reality for manufacturers. In the case of the USA, an RPE of $100,000 USD is handled per employee per year; in the case of Latin America it is $50,000 USD per employee per year.

Rony: **Independence, Absence days,** is the number of days that you, as a CEO and/or founder, can be totally absent from the management of the company. The best way of measuring leadership is with the absence of the leader, so we have to test it. An effective absence is not executing daily activities and delegating functions, so that the company can continue working without the presence of the CEO or his decisions, giving the leadership team the opportunity to make decisions for the sake of the company while the CEO can be on vacations, at a training course somewhere remote, or visiting strategic clients or suppliers. In addition to the benefits the absence of the CEO brings to the company, it gives him the possibility of dealing with unfinished business that is constantly postponed. One of the most effective days for people is the day before they go on vacation. This indicator helps measure the level of dependency of the CEO, and how well prepared the company is in case of an eventuality. The higher the number, the lower the level of dependency from the owner, which implies that the succession can be smoother.

Rony: **Reliability** in percentage of fulfilled objectives. Leadership teams should establish objectives every quarter, which they work

towards during that period of time. How closely your results get to your pre-set goals indicates your ability to carry out your agreements. Likewise, the reliability of the fulfillment of the agreements made with customers, since times are getting shorter and every customer bases their services and products on the internal and delivery times of their suppliers. So, if suppliers don't meet their deliveries on time, they cause inefficiency, chaos and uncertainty.

Dan: Now I understand lots of the questions you asked a few moments ago.

Rony: Tell me, in the last five years, what was your annual revenue and the number of employees you had per year. Also, share with me how many days you could be absent per year, and the level of reliability of objective fulfillment.

Rony: As you can see from the numbers we have, your RPE is low, with a maximum of two absence days from you and 70% reliability.

Year	Revenue	Employees	RPE	Independence	Reliability
2015	$ 1,781,818.00	100	$ 17,818.18	0	Non reliable
2016	$ 2,281,818.00	80	$ 28,522.73	0	Non reliable
2017	$ 2,645,454.00	83	$ 31,872.94	0	Non reliable
2018	$ 2,827,272.00	90	$ 31,414.13	0	Non reliable
2019	$ 3,054,545.00	80	$ 38,181.81	2	50%
2020	$ 3,190,909.00	85	$ 37,540.11	2	70%

You could feel the silence. Dan didn't know what to say. I could see he was uncomfortable analyzing the numbers in front of him. After a couple of minutes, I asked him:

Rony: If you had the chance of investing money into this company now, would you do it?

Dan: If those were the numbers of a company that I'm about to invest money in, I would probably not be motivated. You can see the inefficiency in the RPE, a level of total dependency from the owner, and low fulfillment of agreements. There is a high risk.

Rony: If you align every effort so the company can improve these indicators, what would you have to change?

Dan: This is very enlightening, but at the same time frightening. This information is an eye opener. This can no longer be. I would have to change the way we operate, I should learn how to delegate, be able to be absent and many other things. My head is spinning, I don't even know where to start.

Rony: I think that's why we are having this conversation. After everything we talked about, I can finally tell you that I can help your company. Things don't necessarily have to be as they are.

Dan: I think there should be a different way of doing things, because as they are now, they aren't working correctly.

Rony: It's good that you are not satisfied with things as they are and want to change them! Have you ever used a GPS, Waze or Google maps?

Dan: Yes, of course, unfortunately I am totally dependent on Waze. Wherever I go I use the app to get to my destination faster; I have even forgotten how to get to some places that I knew by heart. I think I actually depend on it.

Rony: What are the steps to use it?

Dan: First, I open the app and type the direction where I want to go and then, it gives me different routes to choose from.

Rony: You are nearly right, the first thing that the app does is to locate your geographical position to understand where you're at, we're calling it point A; when you set the destination, which is point B, the system calculates routes and chooses the one you prefer. If you have a detour, Waze says…

Dan: Recalculating.

Rony: Exactly. That's what we are doing here. We want to understand what your point A is, the origin from where you are standing today as a company and as a businessman. Point B we'll talk about in our next meeting, and from there we'll define the route, which will be measured constantly, and when we have a detour, we'll recalculate a new one.

At that moment, I stood up, and wrote on the flip chart "point A" and the characteristics that the company had at that time, and I told him:

Rony: Summing up, these are the reasons why I believe you feel trapped, and why you have no control over the company: you don't have a leadership team to delegate tasks to. there's no business strategic plan to follow and to which everyone should be aligned: not only are your productivity and efficiency low, but also your clients are unsatisfied with the service you give them. Besides, you don't sleep enough and have problems with your wife because your mind is on the company.

Dan: I couldn't have explained it better.

Rony: You mentioned that your staff isn't committed, tell me more about it.

Dan: I feel people don't care about what's happening here. There are many problems and it all depends on me.

Rony: When I entered the company, I noticed some things were in bad condition, like paint, uniforms, misplaced garbage and chaos at your office.

Dan: Yes, with time things have been piling up and we haven't taken care of the aesthetics of the company. But I don't think my office would be a problem, I don't mind the chaos.

Rony: Company is a reflection of its leader. if the offices are in chaos, it is not congruent to demand that the rest of the organization should be in order. Regarding the "aesthetics," they also have a very important impact. Are you familiar with the broken windows theory?

Dan: No, I have never heard of it.

Rony: **The broken windows theory** originated from an experiment carried out by a psychologist from Stanford University named Philip Zimbardo, in 1969. It consisted of ditching a car in the Bronx neighborhood which was deteriorated at that time: poor, dangerous, conflictive and full of crime. Zimbardo left the vehicle with no license plates and the doors unlocked, just to see what happened. After ten minutes, parts of the car were already stolen little by little. Three days later, nothing of value remained on the car and it was ruined. However, that was only the first part of the experiment. The second part consisted of ditching an identical vehicle, with similar conditions,

in a rich and quiet neighborhood: Palo Alto, California. A week passed and nothing happened to the car. But Zimbardo decided to intervene: he took a hammer and banged on parts of the vehicle, including one of the windows. The car seemed misused and abandoned. So, Zimbardo's hypothesis was confirmed. What happened? From the moment the car was left in bad conditions, Palo Alto's residents did the same thing that the Bronx residents did. This experiment gave birth to the broken windows theory, elaborated by James Wilson and George Kelling: if a building has a broken window which isn't fixed soon, soon the rest of the windows will be broken by vandals.

Dan: It's like when you buy a new car, you keep it intact. When you leave it to valet parking, they take great care of it, but if it has some scratches or a dent, they won't take care of it because they'll think, "If the owner doesn't take care of it, what difference does it make if I don't either? He won't notice".

Rony: The same happens in a company. People will take care of things based on appearance.

Dan: I will take note and handle some of the points you mentioned. I don't want people not taking care of the company because it seems like I'm not taking care of it either. It's just that I was focused on more important things.

Rony: I don't doubt it. For sure you've been working hard on keeping the company alive, but now we have the opportunity to change its culture and results. If you want people to worry, get involved and even passionate about the company, well, that should be reflected in actions more than words.

Dan: As my grandmother used to say, "Your actions speak louder than your words." Duly noted.

Rony: Probably this will be the last question that I have for you today. Why change? Why not leave things as they are and continue managing the company as you already do?

Dan: Because I want to be free, I don't want to live like this anymore, always living in urgency and distress. I want to be able to go on vacations

as my employees do, I want to be able to be absent knowing things will still be executed correctly. I want to have more money and be able to build a legacy for my family.

Rony: At point B, we are going to write: freedom, better control and economic affluence.

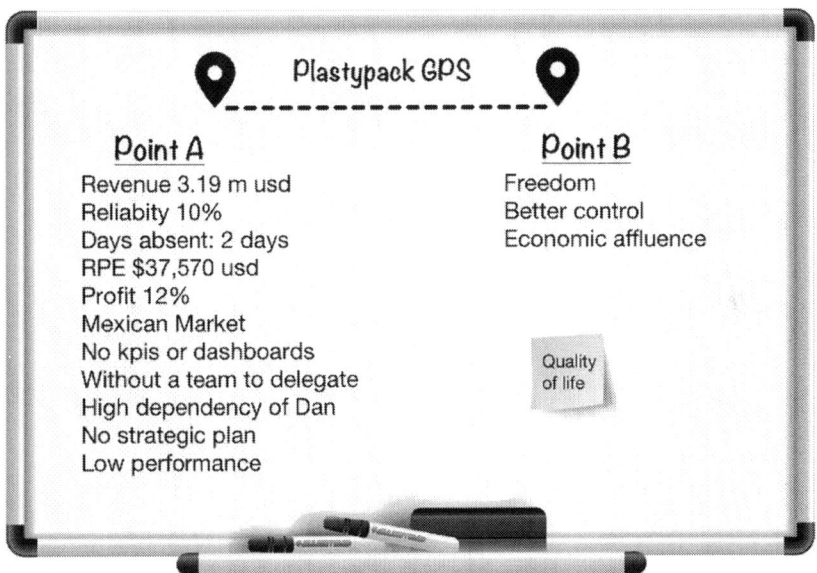

Dan: I like this visual map; it helps me understand where we are and where we are going.

Rony: Perfect. To make our relationship work it is important to fulfill three requirements: a) you are the leader of change and should be involved in the entire process; b) your leadership team will be part of the work process; and c) that you are satisfied knowing that my duty, on one hand, is to train, but also showing you what is not working, which you can feel as a "critic". These three points are not negotiable. If you don't want to involve the team, things will remain as they are now; if you are not the leader of change and your team doesn't feel you are involved in this, they won't be either; and if I don't become your "devil's advocate" showing you or criticizing what is wrong, there is no reason for me to work with you.

Dan: I love it. I expect great honesty from you, to tell me things as they are. I would rather be with people who tell me what I need to hear instead of what I want to hear. What's next?

Rony: Well, I will send you the contract. I need an organizational chart, emails of the people that should make up your leadership team, and of 10 more people; all these people will be in the process of "organizational diagnosis," for which I will send a questionnaire and interview some people. That way I will have the big picture of the company. For now, we'll be meeting alone, as there are some things that we have to set out before involving your directive team.

Conclusions:

❯ At the beginning of every process of organizational change and / or transition, it is very important that you clearly define the point of departure A and the final destination B, as if it were a GPS, having a clear vision of the obstacles that prevent growth, which usually is that "everything depends on the owner".

❯ Remember that the three key indicators of growth and increased value of an organization are: Reliability, RPE (revenue per employee) and independence (leader's absence days).

❯ Once you are clear on where you stand, you can start taking actions to improve things.

2 ESTABLISHING A GROWTH VISION.

> ❱ Alice in wonderland is standing in front of the smiling cat, she asks "Where do these two roads lead?" to which the cat answers, "Where do you want to go?" She says that she doesn't know, so the cat tells her: "If you don't know where you're going then it doesn't matter which road you take."
>
> ❱ If you don't know where you're going, every effort will have mediocre results. How can you lead a team with aligned efforts and have positive results in the company without knowing where you're going?

Rony: It's good to see you again, and thanks for the trust you put in me! I made some progress with the organizational diagnosis. Your staff was very cooperative answering the questionnaires and openly participating in the interviews. Now I have a bigger picture of where the company stands and what we must do.

Dan: What's the result? What do we need to work on?

Rony: I'll sum up what I discovered. There is no business plan. There's a war between departments. There's also an organizational culture of blaming others. There is no way of measuring results objectively. You are your competitors' university, meaning you train people and when they are ready, the competition steals them. You have a high level of personnel turnover. Your cash flow is deficient. You don't have a methodology of working. Nothing is standardized. There are no clear criteria for selection. The decision making is centralized mainly

on you and there is no leadership team. In summary, you don't have a company, you have self-employment where everything depends on you.

Dan: I don't like what I'm hearing, but I understand it. I agree, it is not a business because everything depends on me. It is worse than having a job, because if I was an employee I could go on vacations and not be worried about money or the payroll. If I was an employee, I wouldn't have mortgaged my house to invest capital in the company. I don't like where I'm standing or what I created. I think that's why I'm working with you.

Rony: That's the plan, turning things around, so that you can free the company's potential … and yours. These past few years everyone's selling the fantastic idea of being an entrepreneur, which is amazing and contributes a lot to society. But there is not much content, material and assistance to help companies beyond a Start-up, once they are at the Scale-up phase. Later, I will explain the stages of a company, but for the moment, let's get back to what must be corrected here. To put it graphically, you live in a situation where the tail is wagging the dog, and not the other way around. Meaning, you are at the mercy of the company's needs. Let's turn that around, let the dog wag the tail.

Dan: I love this image. I agree, the dog should wag the tail. I feel like a victim and prisoner of my own company.

Rony: If it makes you feel better, this situation is very common. The transition from a Start-up to Scale-up phase leads to changes of attitude, habits, and ways of making decisions. To put it simply, you are lacking an effective working method.

Dan: Method?

Rony: Yes, **methodologies are proven tools** that accelerate results. As we say in Mexico: "There is no need to invent black thread or wet water, both already exist." There is no need to invent the margarita pizza recipe, but you can use the knowledge and ways of working that have been used before to make margarita pizza; you are repeating a successful formula. The same happens to this new stage of the company. We'll employ a methodology.

Dan: Understood. As a kid, I used to play the piano and I was taught with a methodology that I didn't understand until I wanted to learn to play the guitar. Then I realized that the teaching method was slightly different, and that I could learn the teacher's system easier.

Rony: Well, let's continue to understand where we are standing, which is our point A on the GPS. A bigger picture shows us that we have an organization with low efficiency, without a strategic plan, with high dependency on you, and without a leadership team you can delegate tasks to. There are no dashboards with key performance indicators that illustrate the reality of the organization You have an excessive variety of products, you have a large customer database but you don't know who your ideal core customer is, there is no brand promise, no competitive advantage…

Dan: Stop, stop. I have a stomachache. The worst thing is that with each one of those things I already read them or someone had already told me about them, but at the moment I had no time to change them. People suggested books about nearly every problem you mentioned.

Rony: By any chance, do you have those books piled up with everything or all together on a bookshelf waiting for you to read them and implement some ideas from each one?

Dan: Yes, I honestly have both. At the office I have a bookshelf with some of the suggested books and at home I have a pile of books on my night table.

Rony: The pile of books is known as the "guilty tower". Guilt, because each time we see them, we feel guilty knowing that there's a possible solution, but without time or energy to read them and try to fix things, until we become immune from that guilt and just continue living.

Dan: Exactly. There's no time or energy, but right now I have no choice. This has to change, because it can cost me the mortgaged house, the company, my health and even my marriage.

Rony: Yes, I understand, you are at a moment where your only alternative is to make time to work on and solve each one of the things

that will help you take control of the organization. What would be our point B at the GPS? In other words, the destination where we're going.

Dan: I want my problems to end, so that people can work with less drama, so that I can go on vacations and disconnect from my mobile and not have to travel with the bank token.

Rony: That's a good first step; however, we have to think long-term. What you are describing are requirements of the final destination. Let's use **BHAG**: Big Hairy, Audacious Goal. This term was created by Jim Collins in his book *Build to Last,* where he mentions that long-term objectives should be created to define where you want to be in the next 10 to 30 years. One of the most popular BHAG's, which actually changed our society, was when Bill Gates was leading Microsoft and established as his BHAG "a computer on every desk." You should consider that this happened in the 80's, when computers were exaggeratedly big and expensive. It was crazy to think that could be possible. Not only did he achieve it, but now we all have a computer in our pocket. He set a goal, which he pursued constantly. It was his north star. What happens when you don't know where you want to go? **It is easier to plan from future to present.** If you are clear on where you want to be in the next 30 years, you can define where you're going to be in the next 20, 10, 5 or one year, even in the next quarter. That way, you align priorities, investments, suppliers, efforts, plans, ideas, products, employees and customers towards the same target. It's like the power of a laser: when it's used at high concentration levels it can cut diamonds. BHAG works like point B on the GPS, a very long-term goal.

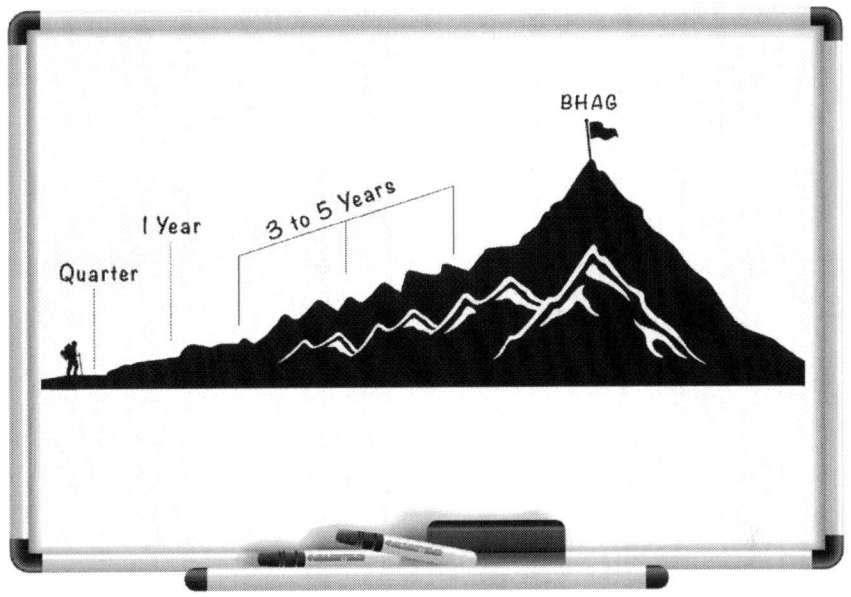

Rony: BHAG is like climbing the Himalayas. You have to plan how you are going up and where you are going to camp. Suppose that your BHAG is for 20 years. We define where we should be in 10 years, then in 3 to 5 years, then 1 year and finally, a quarter. That way the goals we set for the organization's next quarter will be aligned to a long-term objective.

Rony: Some BHAGs that have transformed companies. Google: "organizing the world's information;" Facebook: "connecting the world;" Uber: "reliable transportation like water running everywhere and for everyone;" Tesla: "accelerate world's transition of sustainable energy;" Alibaba: "to ease the power of doing business everywhere;" Evernote: "remember everything;" SpaceX: "making the exploration and settlement on Mars possible." Committing to a long-term objective will simplify your life. You'll be obsessed with walking and measuring the progress towards the important destination, avoiding distractions.

Dan: I understand.

Rony: What's the greatest vision you have for the company? Can you imagine it in 20 or 10 years?

Dan: Honestly, at this moment I can only imagine it for the next three years. The market conditions have changed a lot and my company isn't exactly under my control.

Rony: Perfect. We don't have to establish an objective for 30 years right now. In fact, there are not many companies that can do that. Let's start with what you can see clearly or what you would like to achieve.

Dan: In three years, I would like that the company didn't depend on me anymore, that our annual revenue would be three times of what it is today, that we double our profits, and start operations in Colombia.

Rony: Excellent. It sounds like a brilliant challenge. So, at the moment, we already know our point A. Today we have annual revenue of 3.8 million USD with a profit of 12% and we only operate in Mexico, with a high level of dependency from you. In three years, you want to have an annual revenue of 9.5 million USD with a profit of 24% and operations in both Mexico and Colombia, counting on your participation but not on your dependency. You don't have to have a good memory; you only need to set a long-term objective and reflect on paper the different phases to achieve that objective.

Dan: That's very good! Because I don't have a good memory. What worries me a little is if I want to change BHAG along the way. What happens if I'm walking in the wrong direction?

Rony: I don't know if it's the wrong direction, but it is better to walk towards a specific direction than walking nowhere. Besides, you are establishing the objectives, so they are not written in stone. You can change them, but I do recommend you commit to your BHAG. It is possible that at the end of this year, you realize this BHAG is short and you can see past it. So, we start walking towards your desired destination. If that's where we want to be in three years, what should we achieve next year?

Dan: Following the same line, we should have an annual revenue of 4.09 million USD; that implies an increase of 28% in our sales, and our profit should be at least 16%. Regarding my dependency, I would like to be able to go on vacations with my family for two weeks without

being linked to the company; my wife wants to kill me each time we go on vacations and I'm not present to live experiences with my children.

Rony: Exactly, "happy wife happy life". Everything is clearer now. And to achieve next year's objective, where should we be standing in three months?

Dan: This quarter, sales should reach 1.59 million USD. It is our strongest season and I have to make good use of that. I would like to have 15% profit. That percentage would show some progress. And for me, I'm not sure, can you suggest something?

Rony: Of course. I suggest that this quarter we set as an objective having a leadership team that works based on a dashboard. That way you'll have more visibility and clarity.

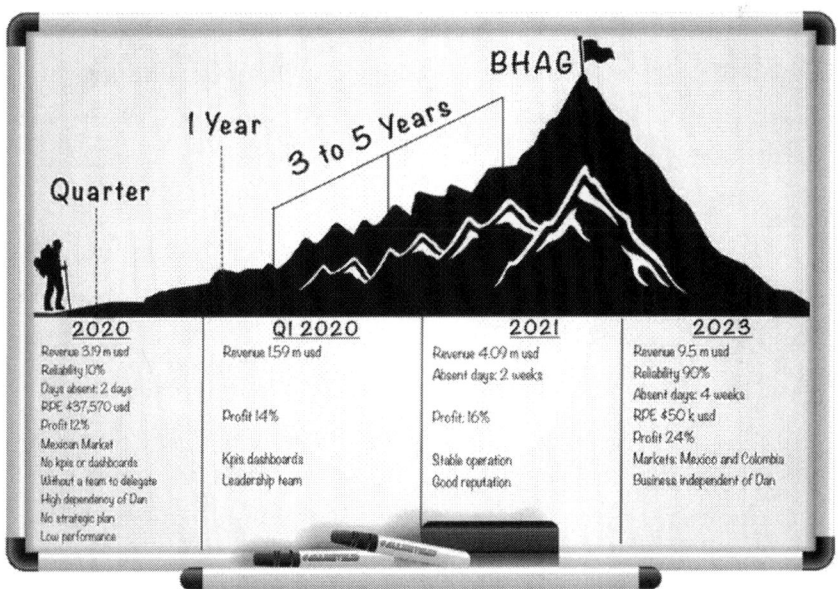

Dan: I like the idea.

Rony: I ask you to write these goals on the flip chart, which could also be at your office, where you can see them every day, and that you write your BHAG on a piece of paper which you can put on your wallet. We are taking advantage of your Reticular Activating System (RAS).

Dan: Reticular acti... what?

Rony: The **Reticular Activating System** is the brain's attention center. The key to "turning on the brain". Someone can program the reticular active system on purpose choosing the exact messages that are sent consciously. For example, when you want to buy a white Honda, surprisingly you start to find white Hondas on the street. Second, your reticular activating system can't distinguish between "real events" and "synthetic". In other words, you tend to believe in any message you give it. Imagine you are going to give a speech; you can practice by visualizing it in your mind. This "simulation" practice improves the way you'll deliver the speech.

Dan: I remember when Andrea, my wife, was pregnant, she saw pregnant women everywhere. The same happened when we wanted to buy our apartment, I started finding advertisements everywhere. One day, as a joke, I asked Andrea if those advertisements were placed for us on purpose.

Rony: Establishing a goal works, somehow, because we establish our RAS to pay attention to the things that will help us reach that goal! RAS works like that, whether it was programmed on purpose or not. Establishing goals and thinking about them every day helps programming your RAS, to put attention on the things that will support your goal.

Dan: I like it, but I have to admit I'm starting to feel frightened.

Rony: That's a good sign. Remember that it is named BHAG, and the H stands for "Hairy", that is fear. Fear implies you are getting out of your comfort zone, that you dare to go beyond your limits. It's better to set a goal than not to have one. Most people avoid establishing goals because they fear failing. I can assure you that not settling a goal won't avoid failing, you just won't notice it. It is better to establish a goal and work to achieve it; in case of failure, you didn't really fail, you progressed towards a specific destination. For me, failure is making mistakes and not learning from them.

Dan: As Nelson Mandela said: "I never lose, either I win or I learn."

Rony: So, let's use that fear on your behalf, as an advisor and not as a jailer.

Dan: I like that. Let me write it down so I won't forget it. It's a good motto "let fear be an advisor and not a jailer." But having an objective will limit me.

Rony: Boundaries are good, they simplify our lives. When someone is vegetarian, that person apparently has limited things to eat and might seem to have a complicated life, but in reality, his life is simpler. For example, if he goes to the Cheesecake Factory, instead of reading the entire menu for hours, he only has to search or ask the waiter for vegetarian options.

Dan: Yes, that's an endless menu. When I finish reading it, I don't remember what I wanted to order and have to start reading it over again. It's frustrating.

Rony: That's right. Boundaries help simplify your decision making, because you only have to make decisions from a selected group of things. Like when you are browsing through Netflix to see the pool of movies it has, you can spend at least an hour searching what you want to watch, and at the end, you can't even remember which movie caught your attention. If on the search engine you set a limit for action movies, it helps you simplify your decision making. First, you have to imagine what you want to create, commit and make a plan to achieve it, take action, measure the results and adjust them along the way.

Dan: That sounds like "the law of attraction" or the movie *The secret*.

Rony: Well, it's not far from it, we are talking about the same thing, but knowing that it's not enough to only think or wish for it, because it won't magically come true. We actually have to work to make it happen. Having a clear vision of what you want to achieve helps, but think about it every-day and work to make it happen. The great majority of people prefer not to establish an objective because it implies a commitment and possibly failure. The irony here is that if you don't have goals, you won't be able to feel successful. By the way, what is your definition of success?

Dan: Success would be to be recognized as a great businessman, have a lot of money, travel in first class, and give talks about my life story.

Rony: I had a similar definition, until I discovered that it was making my life miserable, so I learned about Earl Nightingale's philosophy: "Success is the progressive realization of a worthy goal or ideal." It sounds simple, but gradual progress gives a sensation of success. You can feel successful today with the current conditions you have. You only have to feel you're making progress.

Dan: I don't understand that.

Rony: Have you ever been on a diet, wanting to improve your physical condition?

Dan: Who hasn't?

Rony: Exactly. Each day is a battle for eating healthy and exercising. Each accomplished day is a victory, and when days of victory pass, your self-esteem increases, you feel better, more confident; and much better when the scale or your clothes confirm the results. Each time you achieve more progress towards your objective, you should feel…

Dan: Successful!!! I got it. It seemed like a mediocre definition, but with it I have the opportunity of feeling good today and achieving my results. With my former definition of success, I only felt frustrated. I will put this new one into practice.

Rony: Part of the process that we are working with leads to a deep change of ideas, beliefs and definitions, above all, yours. Because you are the one who will make a greater impact on the organization. Every company is a reflection of its leader. Changing ideas or beliefs is the key in the development of an organization because it means that you have evolved. If the company changes, it is because you did.

Dan: It's so hard, it gives me a headache to think so differently.

Rony: Yes, change is painful. It's like when a bone is broken and wasn't set correctly, so it has to be broken again to be set properly. People say it hurts more breaking it again than it did when it did the first time.

Dan: Yes, it's awful!!!

Rony: Well, at this company some bones have been wrongly set, so we have to break them again to reset them. I didn't promise the process was going to be painless, I promised it was going to be improved. In the process you'll feel pain, but it won't last. The good thing is that we are moving forward with the process. We know clearly the reality of the company. You are not fighting ghosts anymore. Now they have names, therefore, solutions. We also know where we're going. Albert Einstein used to say to his students that if he had one hour to solve a world's problem, he would use 55 minutes to analyze the problem and reach an accurate diagnosis, and once knowing the source, it would take him 5 minutes to find a solution. The GPS is our diagnosis. We know where we're standing and where we're going. To have clarity helps enormously in making a decision with the greatest amount of information.

It is very common for company leaders to feel frustrated because people aren't aligned, don't work on the same objective, and have many communication problems. The irony is that the CEO hasn't created that common objective and / or people interpreted it differently; either way it is his responsibility to establish it and explain it to people. If you want people to be on the same page, you have to create the page. That's what we are doing.

Dan: Honestly, that would be good for me too, because I often change objectives. My wife says that I never commit to an objective. I swear, it's not a lack of commitment, it's just that other things become more urgent.

Rony: Aren't you tired of living with urgencies?

Dan: Yes, very. It even seems like I'm a firefighter, putting out fires all the time.

Rony: Anthony Robbins says, "The road to somewhere leads to nowhere," so it's better to establish a specific objective. If you are clear that your goal is to start operations in Colombia, are there activities, products, suppliers that come to your mind that need to be eliminated and others that should be incorporated?

Dan: Yes, of course. I should start networking with Colombia's chamber of commerce and eliminate my payroll supplier. I don't see how he could help in that vision.

Rony: Excellent. You are starting to know what having clear goals is. In this case, without remorse, you can say NO to those things that distract you.

Have you ever noticed how countries that have a vision and strategic plan are much more evolved and have better quality of life? For example, Anglo-Saxon countries like the USA and England have a vision and a long-term plan. They work for common well-being and achieving plans as a nation. They think ahead for the next 40 or 60 years. Unfortunately, it is not the case of Mexico and Latin America. we think at most in the next 4 years. Each time a new president wins, it seems like the computer resets and everything starts from scratch. There is no long-term plan. So, as you can see, having a vision helps in a great measure.

Now's the time for you to start involving your team in the process. It's important that you gather with them and explain to them the GPS, Point A, current situation, and Point B, the objective you want to reach as a company.

Dan: But what happens if they don't buy the idea, or don't like the vision?

Rony: There are many options: a) you can try and sell the idea better; b) you listen to their feedback, because maybe they can help you have something better; c) you don't have the right people and it's better for you that they leave the ship as soon as possible.

Dan: Looking at it like that, it's simple. I hope everyone gets on the ship.

Rony: It is normal if you feel resistance. People don't like change; they would rather live in their comfort zone even though it is not that comfortable. When you feel more resistance, it will be at the time when we implement KPI dashboard where we are going to measure people's results. Then you'll see their inconvenience and that they prefer the former working method: NO METHOD.

Conclusions:

- Defining the destination point as clearly as possible helps you to understand the team, tools, resources, etc., that you need to arrive at the final destination, because if you don't plan where you're going, you probably won't arrive.

- Once you have your point of destination make sure that everyone understands the same things, that the language they speak at your organization is consistent and coherent.

3 SPEAKING A COMMON LANGUAGE.

> Berlitz's advertisement shows amusingly that language is the key to effective communication. In the video you can see how at a German control tower, where the US coast guard makes an emergency call saying, "We are sinking!", and the operator answers "What are you thinking about?".

> Each community has a particular language, with its denominations and slangs. But, if the terms aren't clear, people will understand different things from a single statement.

We met at David's office, another one of my clients whose process is more advanced, as we have come a long way. David can share his experience, but in particular the problem and chaos that he experienced when a fundamental part of the company isn't right. I mean, specifically, the language. We stayed for a few minutes talking in the parking lot before going up to David's office.

Rony: What would you say if you only had 60 seconds to negotiate the life of a person who's been kidnapped by a terrorist?

Dan: Mm. Oh, I don't know. How hard!

Rony: Chriss Voss is a former agent of the FBI that used to negotiate on behalf of hostages Today, he is the CEO of The Black Swan Group. He not only travels around the world making risky hostage negotiations, but also teaching entrepreneurs how to negotiate correctly. He says the key is the kind of language he uses, because each word has an emotional impact. When he is negotiating with a terrorist, he shouldn't use the

tools of active listening, which make you say things like "I understand that you're angry", "I can sense you're angry." Instead, you should say "apparently you are upset and tired of this situation…" The way you talk determines the kind of negotiation you can achieve.

Dan: Wow! I can imagine the kind of training they need to have the power of having such sensitive conversations.

Rony: From what he explains, he focuses on speaking the right language to generate the right empathy. Let's get inside David's office, so you can meet him and listen to his experience through his process and the impact of language.

David: It is very nice meeting you Dan, you are in good hands with Rony and his team. He has helped us a lot in our scaling process.

Rony: I would like if you to share your experience about common language. The constant conflict you had for "not talking the same language."

Dan: Thanks for having us, although, I think at my company we all talk the same language.

David: I think you are going to be surprised. I also thought we talked the **same language**, but with Rony's help we realized we didn't. While some were talking about a specific term, to others it meant something else. I was frustrated because my team wasn't communicating easily and because each person interpreted things differently. For example: I asked to be informed on sales progress, for which I asked for the invoiced amount. For me it was obvious that everyone understood what invoicing is, but they gave me the information of customer purchase orders, which is not the same thing: one leads to the other, but they aren't the same. It also happened that while someone in my team talked about our core customer, he was really talking about the consumer, because we weren't clear about the difference between core customer and consumer.

Dan: I don't understand. Aren't consumers and customers the same thing?

Rony: Not necessarily. It depends on the product, service and company. There is no general rule. To define it easily, a customer is

the one whose needs you must satisfy and as a result he is willing to pay a price for the value he gets from us. The consumer is the one who consumes the product. Occasionally, both are the same person, but not always. For example, Nestlé's customers, specifically on cereals, are larger supermarkets, and the consumers are mainly mothers that worry about the health and well-being of their children. Those mothers are the customers of Nestlé's customers, and of course their opinions and satisfaction have an impact, but Nestlé should be focused on satisfying the supermarket. On the next level, the mother is the customer and children the consumers.

David: In our case, we have two product lines. It took us time to understand the difference between customer and consumer with each product. We thought it was generic but it was formulated wrong, which made us feel very stressed. We are a call center, where we receive many calls. At the beginning, we thought that our clients were the people who called us; but with Rony's help, we understood that our clients are professionals that pay for advertisements, and thanks to those advertisements people call us to where we gather data and assign appointments with our consumers Those who called are the customers of our customers. Now we understand we have to make our customers happy and distinguish who gives the feedback, because it has a different weight and importance. It is not the same to have feedback from a regular customer than from a "Top 10 customer."

Rony: We haven't got there yet with Dan. We haven't categorized customers, but do me a favor and please explain to him what "Top 10" means.

David: Top 10 are the most important 10 customers that we have, whose satisfaction weighs more than that of any other customer, because they're the ones who keep the organization alive. Those are our ideal customers, that we want to keep and replicate.

Dan: So, have you discovered many differences in language?

David: Many. I started my company with three people. Now we're a company of 160 people. I assumed everyone understood what I asked for and said, but it wasn't happening, and that frustrated me a lot.

Apparently, language was only clear for me: I asked for profit reports and people gave me the revenue, I asked for the available installed capacity to meet new customers, and each one gave me different numbers and perspectives. Not only did we have different perceptions, but the numbers were different.

Rony: As you can see, Dan, it is very common that people assume everyone understands. The human brain uses the "function" of assumption to avoid processing a lot of constant information. However, in business we have to avoid people assuming things and we should be as clear as possible, to avoid confusion and / or good intentions. A while ago, one of my mentors, David Chavez, taught me a funny way to understand the meaning of the word ASSUME. If you divide the word ASS/U/ME, it represents the "Ass between U and Me." Assuming it is very dangerous.

Dan: But how can people understand the same message that is mentioned in the company differently?

David: Because each person comes from a different background, and has different knowledge, and has never worked at your company. It is your responsibility to train people with your process and language.

Rony: I'm not sure if I told you this, but communication is the most common complaint from people involved in scaling up companies. Let me tell you that communication is not the problem, it's everything underneath it. Communication is the evidence when things aren't working. It's like only seeing the tip of the iceberg. Underneath there are all the issues with wrong processes, methodologies, indicators, policies, language, etc. Whenever I go to England for workshops or meetings, a very common misunderstanding that happens when we talk about figures, for example, is that when we say: "a billion," which in the US is actually a thousand million, or a biscuit for them is a cookie and for us a bun. The word pants for them means underwear, and so on with many other words.

Dan: Now that I remember, once I went to work in the UK, and I got to the building where my meeting was taking place, which was on the first floor. So, I was at the ground floor, which for us in the US is the first

floor, and couldn't find the meeting room so I had to call the person that I was meeting and ask him if I was at the wrong building or if I had the wrong time or date because I couldn't find the meeting room. He laughed and said: "Here in the UK the first floor is what would be the second floor in the US." We both laughed and then I found the meeting room.

The three of us laughed a lot because of the story. These situations where words mean different things because of the geographic location of where they're said have happened to all of us.

Rony: Words have different meanings depending on the place and education. It's your responsibility to establish a **"dictionary" at your company**, to make sure people speak the language that you want, even though these people belong to the same country and region as you do. My wife and I belong to nearly the same social circle, but at her parents' house "we need to talk" meant "we have something unresolved and we have to solve it," while at my house it meant "I did something wrong and I was going to be punished for it."

Dan: Yes, I grew up the same way as you did.

Rony: With this example you'll see how language can make an impact on the confusion and drama of an organization. With this "riddle" you'll have different answers: If I had four eggs, and a thief gave me three and my rooster laid five more, how many do I have?

Dan: Let me count. I would say six eggs, the four that you had already minus three that the thief took plus five the cockerel laid.

David: I would say seven eggs. The four you had and the thief brings three.

Dan: And what about the other five from the rooster?

Rony: The rooster doesn't lay eggs, the hen does. Imagine if you ask this riddle to your team, how many different answers do you think you'll have at your companies?

Dan: Well, we are five, so at least four different answers.

Rony: See? Everything starts with language. Some words have the same root or are even written or spoken exactly the same but mean different things.

Dan: I am asking myself how much confusion exists already in my organization because of language differences.

David: You can't even begin to imagine. My biggest conflict with my team is that people can understand and correctly reply to the question of "how much did we earn this quarter?". For me, earnings are the total profit of a period of time, but some of my team members thought the money we earned was what we had in our invoices, while others thought it was the income we had in our bank account. We had three different answers for the same question.

Dan: And what should I do? I'm worried already. Something similar happens to me. I ask something and people reply with something different from what I wanted to hear. Nowadays, with so many questions sent by email or Whatsapp, I can't see how people react to know if they understood correctly.

Rony: What should you do? Make a dictionary for your company.

Dan: A dictionary for my company?

David: Yes, look, this is the dictionary of my company. When a new person starts working with us, part of his training process consists of the terms and language that we use at the company. We don't assume people understand what we want to say, rather we teach them instead of living with constant confusions and conflicts.

Dan: It sounds interesting, and how can I make and implement this dictionary?

Rony: First, gather your team and make a list of the terms that are commonly used at your company. Then, discuss the meaning of each one of them. Once you agree with a conclusion or definition write it down. The dictionary is a document that should be updated from time to time. You may change definitions that once were apparently correct. Only time will decide what is right or wrong.

David: Only having a team discussion will help clarifying things and lowering communication barriers among team members.

Rony: Business Coaches have a special training where we can identify different levels of language. The way people talk has a high

impact on what they think and how they act. For example, it's not the same when a person says: "I have to take the inventory" rather than "I should take the inventory" or "I want to take the inventory". Apparently, the three statements are the same, but that's only superficial. If you listen carefully and pay more attention, "have to" means an obligation; "should" has to do with something important, and "want" is doing something only because you feel like it. If you don't believe me, change the word "inventory" for "workout" from the statements I just told you. See how the meaning and energy change.

Dan: I see, it's true. "I want to work out" isn't the same as "I have to work out." "Want" is because you like it, "have to" is because you are obliged.

Rony: Now let's go deeper. The language that people frequently use portrays where they live, whether they feel part of a team or not, and also whether they're happy with their lives. Dave Logan, in his studies and book *Tribal Leadership*, explains that groups of people are like little tribes, each one with its own culture and language depending on the stage they are in. **There are five stages.** While I explain them, identify who is in each stage.

Dan: I'll take notes.

David: I think this will be a good reminder. We did this a while ago. Surely I can understand things better now. It's like watching a movie or reading a book for the second time, you find different things.

Rony: **Stage 1** is called "Life sucks." This represents 2% of the world's population. A tribe in stage 1 lives in a hostile environment. People with stage 1 mindset feel that life is cruel and unjust. They often think that they need to be violent or hateful to survive. It's highly recommended NOT to hire people with this mindset. It will damage the culture of the organization and generate a hostile environment.

Dan: I think I have a couple of stage 1 people at the company that always disagree with everything, without foundation. They are unhappy and nobody wants to work with them.

Rony: **Stage 2,** "My life sucks." This represents 25% of the population.

Dan: And that's better?

David: Sure! Because it is not the same to think that everything's wrong as thinking YOUR life is bad. If MY life's bad, I can accept there are people with better lives than me.

Rony: Also, consider that people, according to the stage they're at, attract similar people. The second stage is characterized by apathy: people with this mindset don't think *life itself* is awful, only *their life*. They don't think that their situation can improve, so they avoid responsibility at all costs. It frequently happens in highly bureaucratic environments, where people have boring and repetitive jobs. Probably they'll blame the boss, the system, or their education for the fact that they can't be more creative. Employees won't show initiative unless they have to.

Dan: At some point in my life I felt like that. I wasn't the best person to hang out with. The good thing is that circumstances changed and I don't feel like that anymore.

David: Everyone has experienced something similar and from time to time we tend to go back to some stages. The good thing about having stages is that they help you identify where you are and where people around you are too.

Rony: **The third stage** is called "I'm great, but you're not." That's the most common mindset, and it affects 48% of the population. Unfortunately, it's still negative and unhealthy, but much better than the first stages. It is characterized by selfishness and arrogance towards others. People with stage 3 mindset only worry about their own interests. They'll bond with both sides of stage 3 people (selfish or arrogant), but only if they both benefit directly. An employee with a stage 3 mindset probably feels lonely, mainly because they often think their colleges are incompetent or lazy. For example, a doctor once said to Dave Logan, the author of the book we are talking about, that nurses are only nurses because they are not intelligent enough or working hard enough to be doctors. Consider how lonely this doctor must feel: he thinks his colleagues lack intelligence and are not as dedicated as he is to appreciate his work. His attitude declares he's in stage 3, and it's

not only unpleasant for his colleagues but it also affects him directly. A tribal stage of culture 3 makes the workplace unproductive, because it prevents real cooperation between members. Individual employees can benefit at stage 3, but good collaboration is necessary to succeed in any significant project, and the employers of this stage are generally very interested in collaborating.

David: With the doctor's example, if he doesn't trust his colleagues enough to delegate responsibilities to them, he won't have time to work on his daily routine tasks, or simply won't be able to perform a surgery, because he is obviously demonstrating distrust of his team.

Rony: To fulfill a significant objective like that by yourself is really hard: it requires help from others. A stage 3 mindset can block the cooperation needed at any thriving company.

Dan: But, from what I can see, stage 3 is better than the others.

Rony: **Stage 4** is called "We are great." It represents 22% of the population. This is the stage we should aspire to. It's an environment of collaborative work and common vision, and what matters the most are group results and common good. A regular question for the members at this stage is: what's better for the company? They make decisions based on the answer to that question. The members of this tribe are united towards common values and a noble cause in which they really believe. The members are more dedicated to the cause of the tribe than to their own success. This healthy collaboration and commitment makes the stage 4 work environment the most successful. The power of making good use of the ideas of every member smooths the path to real innovation.

Dan: Definiely, we are on stage 3. I identified more characteristics of stage 3 in my team than of stage 4.

Rony: For example, in 2003 IDEO designed some new buildings for the *Kaiser Permanente* hospital group. Before they started, they worked together with Kaiser's team playing roles, asking them to act as if they were patients. By doing that, they discovered the new buildings were unnecessary: it was better to rearrange the space they already had. They

kept their value of focusing on patients over their wish of expansion and collaborated to find a better solution.

David: Now that we know this, when we hire people we look for at least a stage 3 mindset, and help them evolve to stage 4. I pay extra attention to the people who say "me" instead of "we". I want to eradicate individual mindset and promote group mindset. I want customers to see us as a united company and not divided by departments.

Rony: **Stage 5** is called "Life is great", it represents 2% of the population. Is the rarest of stages, almost uthopic (utopian?). Only a few tribes arrive at this stage and for a very short period of time; later they go back to stage 4. At stage 5, the central cause of the tribe is the only thing that matters to the members. They don't work to fulfill company objectives for personal benefit. Instead, they are amazed by their cause and by the possibilities it offers; to the point where they don't see other companies of the same industry as competition, these companies complement their mission. For example, Amgen biotechnology company was very successful in 1990. When people asked who their biggest competitor was they didn't give the name of another company, but mentioned toxic habits of their own. They didn't aspire to become the most successful corporation in its field; instead, they really wanted to defeat the adversaries of cancer and obesity.

Dan: This is very interesting and a good guide. Definitely we are at stage 3. How can we get to stage 4?

Rony: You should be a stage 4 leader, be an example for your team, generate a common language and objectives that can only be reached with collaborative effort and work, not by themselves but with the support of their fellow team members, to complement your question: what's best for the company? But let's start with those examples.

David: Now, with this review, I realize how much we have progressed. Today I have a team that instead of making excuses or fighting with each other to determine who's right, has become more humble, learned to ask for help and to get it too. My team is more preoccupied with achieving results as a company than with shining individually, as they did before.

Dan: At my company, there's confusion because, for example: someone who works at Sales talks about prices without clarifying whether it's the final price; someone from Production talks about theoretical installed capacity instead of real capacity, which leads to planning and commercial strategy issues; someone from the Finance department talks about the invoiced amount instead of the amount of account receivables. For example, Carlos, a member of the Sales department, registers percentages as indicators, when his objective is to register the quantity of sold pieces. Sadly, we don't have a correct organizational language that promotes success instead of chaos.

Conclusions:

- If you promote and teach the right language at your organization, you will avoid much drama and confusion, which will help you make better decisions in less time.

- Language and problems related to it are linked to the stage where the organization is at the moment.

4 ORGANIZATIONAL STAGES AND TOXIC HABITS.

> ❯ Humans behave according to the stage they're living in, and the same happens with organizations. There are habits and behaviors that are right for the specific moment they are in, and others are destructive because they belong to previous stages.

Rony: Companies are living organisms with predictable behaviors. The company's behavior helps anticipate the next move. As human beings, we live in different stages with adequate behaviors for each one, so any behavior from another stage would be inadequate. These behaviors are known as habits. For example, if a 2-year-old kid interrupts our meeting by entering and burping, what would we do?

Dan: We'd probably laugh.

Rony: What happens if your best salesman is the person who enters and burps?

Dan: I don't know, it would be very uncomfortable and inappropriate.

Rony: That's precisely what I mean. It wouldn't be right because that kind of behavior doesn't correspond to that age. The same happens at companies. For each stage there's an internal behavior that promotes habits and activities. We shall understand in which stage we are and the habits we have and try to find the habits that are right for the moment.

Dan: But, why do I have to find out what's happening inside the company while the competitor is gaining more clients?

Rony: Why is the competitor worrying you if apparently the enemy is inside your house? Departments aren't supporting each other,

managers conspire to blame each other. First, we have to fix what's inside, then we can worry about the competitor. You only have to be a little bit different and better, have a competitive advantage and make the best use of it. There are two indicators that can pinpoint at which stage the company is and the problems it has: number of employees and RPE. Here are the stages of organization according to Daniel Priestly's model:

- **Start-up.** Every business starts with a brilliant concept in someone's mind, with pre-launching enthusiasm and nervousness. While working with ideas, plans, prototypes and groups of abilities, someone created a vision, expecting financial rewards, a more significant job and more freedom.

- **Wilderness** (1-2 founders). After launching, most companies are in a survival mode, which means the founders are working alone. There is no sales team, no one who provides a service or helps with daily operations. The owners don't have much free time, money or liberty. They swing between stress and boredom, often feeling lost and incapable of finding a way of breaking this cycle. In the UK, USA and Australia, 75% of companies don't reach the point where they can start hiring people.

- **Struggle boutique** (3-12 people with low revenue per person). A small team starts to take shape and roles become centralized. The boutique can pay basic salaries while in trouble, but it's not profitable. It's defined by geography (for example, Brighton Pizza Shop, Tampa Bay Printing) and it doesn't develop many assets; the exchange of time is for money.

- **Lifestyle boutique** (3-12 people with high revenue per person). A small and dynamic team with relatively low expenses, with a shaped culture of high energy. The team auto-organizes, enjoys developing digital assets that reach people around the world and the company seems bigger than it actually is. The owner gets higher revenue from what he could gain from a corporate job with more freedom, more impact and less stress. These companies often center on "key influence people" who are known, appreciated and trusted in their industry.

- **The desert** (13-40 people). During this phase of expansion, the company gets too big to be a little boutique and too small to be a great business. General expenses increase with additional staff hiring and growth investment. The company requires leaders, managers, and engineers, but can't afford to pay for these roles. Even though the fundamental business is solid, it stops being profitable and stops investing in long-term projects. It kills cash flow. Culture is damaged when thrown in two directions: plain structure from the past and professional culture from the future. It needs to grow or to reduce quickly before it runs out of cash.

- **The factory** (more than 40 people with low revenue per person). Adding a high number of employees without improving the revenue per person creates a stressful workplace, known as "factory". The company is always on the edge of a financial cliff as the payroll moves forward month to month. There is no money to compensate people for high performance so they leave, and there is no money either for research and development, so things get stuck. The company enters a cycle of cutting down expenses and undermines the active products it once had.

- **Performance** (40-150 people with high revenue per person). A dynamic team of professionals that work with high quality commercial assets. The company is almost unrecognizable from the "lifestyle boutique" that it used to be. The culture, brand, systems, and products have changed, and the company provides services to more markets and territories. They have healthy benefits from well developed strategic assets (mainly digital and intangible). The owners can enjoy the profits or rely on a life changing amount of money.

- **Unicorn** (more than 250 people with super high revenue per person). This is the performance team that was at the right place and time, with the right opportunity and with access to a large amount of funds, like Facebook, Uber, Tesla and LinkedIn. Gets a lot of attention and achieves high rates in a short period of time. These companies are almost impossible to replicate, even though there are millions of people trying.

❶ **Corporation** (more than 250 employees and well established in the market). This great beast of established bureaucracy has many assets and people working to improve them. Corporations used to enjoy a golden position because there were not many things that could dethrone a scaling and strong global business. But recently, each corporation has had to think like an entrepreneur team or risk being interrupted by a fast growing company or an unexpected unicorn. The money that flows around corporations is now fair game for other ambitious corporate teams.

Knowing these predictable stages guides you towards taking actions to have the company you desire.

Dan: I get it, I think we are between factory and performance.

Rony: Right, and both are my specialty. This stage is also known as Scale-up. The initiator of the Scale up trend is Verne Harnish. He is one of my teachers and taught me countless tools he used to transform companies, allowing me to get International Gazelles Coach Certification.

Dan: I remember I read Verne's book Mastering Rockefeller Habits. It was an eye opener and helped me implement a couple of things at the company, but then I forgot about them.

Rony: I also had the fortune of working at Nestlé with Ichak Adizes, who is the organizational corporate transformation guru. He mapped the corporate life cycle, in which the **Go-Go** stage defines Plastypack. Adizes would say that Go-Go companies already have a successful product or service that scales quickly on sales and has strong cash flow. These companies are not only surviving, but also blooming. The key customers are very happy with the products and want more and more. Even investors are starting to get excited. With this success, everybody forgets Infancy tribulations. Constant success can quickly transform confidence into arrogance, with capital A. Go-Go's are susceptible to changing fast and to trying to cover too much. They can't pay attention to specific things because there are too many. They have to make

decisions and commitments that they have never made before and sail into the unknown.

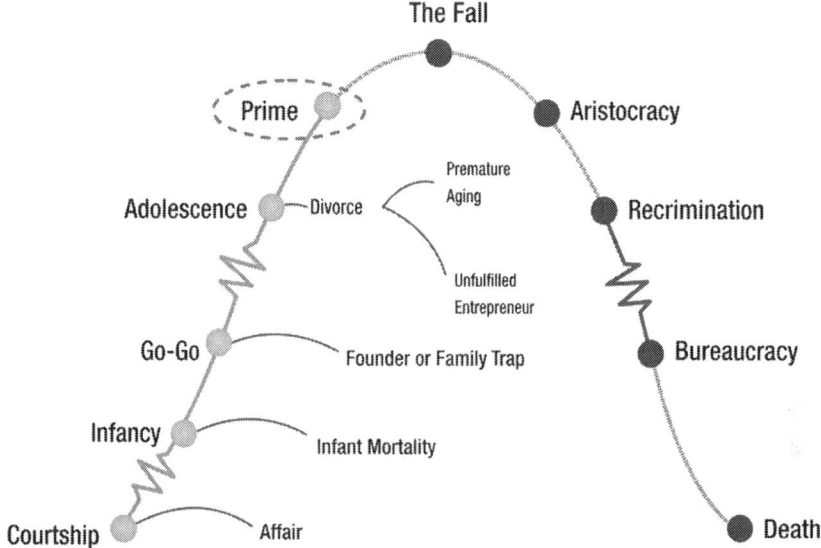

Dan: These three perspectives define my company: We are a Go-Go company from Adizes methodology; a Scale-up company from Harnish philosophy, and a performance company from Priestly's studies.

Rony: This stage frequently presents a series of "toxic habits" or habits that aren't appropriate. I'm going to share them with you. In the meantime, take notes from the ones you identify with, or better yet, write down an example that portrays a bad habit at the organization. For practical ends we'll call them TH (Toxic Habits).

- ❥ **TH1: Setting a bad example.** The organization is a reflection of the leader and his team; ironically, what they complain about is what they provoke. We have to understand what's triggering that kind of behavior in the company. The leader sets the example. For example, if people aren't delivering results it's probably because the owner or the leadership team never demanded such results and the staff isn't focusing on reaching goals. That's why I insist that a company's toxic habits, almost every time, start and end with the leadership team, even if in some cases they are generated by external agents.

❱ TH2: The flavor of the month. This symptom reflects the behavior of the owner of a company that constantly goes to training, reads books, articles and all kinds of information about trends and methodologies. If any idea seems original or appropriate he wants to implement it immediately in his company. For example: the owner reads a book named *Profit First,* arrives at the organization and tells everyone to stop doing what they are doing because from now on, they have to ensure the profitability of the company. Two weeks later, he discovers the book *Blue Ocean Strategy* and tells his team to stop doing what he said before because now the most important thing they have to work on is the competitive advantage to distinguish themselves from the competition. Although it is essential that the owner is well informed and always updating his knowledge, it is also true that constant change drives the team crazy. The team knows that in a couple weeks priorities will change and they will reach a point of not trusting the owner. It becomes like the dynamic of Peter and the wolf or the Boy who cried wolf. What's trending will last until a new trend arrives. Not only does the team not function with this vicious cycle, they also won't commit or progress because they know priorities will change in a few days so there's no need for putting any effort on doing something and finishing it.

❱ TH3: Lack of plan adjustment. It's when the team takes two steps forward and four steps back. It's the kind of behavior of making plans and mistakes without correcting them because the organization has no way of measuring or registering such mistakes. It happens more often at well-established organizations because mistakes get lost in results. However, when the company is in crisis, these mistakes stand out and must be addressed without plans, processes, or habits to obtain the desired result.

❱ TH4: Analysis vs Paralysis. This refers to a directive team that is always planning, never dares to execute, and make mistakes. They focus a lot on planning and don't make decisions. They talk a lot about the long-term future while losing focus on the actual situation, which prevents them from taking actions. They just analyze situations.

- **TH5: Excusitis.** Living in an environment of excuses, which Jacob Neuman, consultant and trainer named it "galloping schizophrenia," consists of blaming others for what's not being solved inside the organization. Organizations live with a great number of absurdities and excuses: "The traffic…", "The climate…", "Someone didn't deliver something on time…", "I didn't get the memo…"; among justifications, objectives get lost. According to a proverb "Explanation given without being asked is a **Justification.**"

- **TH6: Delegation pendulum.** Delegation is an acquired ability but is never taught properly. At MBA there are no lessons on delegation, even though it is an essential quality that helps the leader fulfill results with the help of his team. It is known as pendulum, because by developing this ability the leader can go to one of the two ends of the pendulum, which are: micromanagement or abdication. Micromanagement is supervising and putting a lot of attention to each detail that has been delegated to someone, to the point of checking every email to see if words are written correctly; the person to whom the task was delegated can't make decisions because everything has to pass through the eyes of the supervisor. The opposite happens with abdication, which means not caring for the activities, and trusting blindly in the person to whom the task was delegated without supervising them or getting feedback from them.

- **TH7: Dysfunctional team.** Group members don't work synchronized or with a common objective, which provokes countless consequences that can generally show up as "communication issues", even if that's not the real problem. They are dysfunctional because they don't meet the five levels that Patrick Lencioni found: 1) lack of trust in one another, 2) non-constructive conflicts or lack of debate, 3) lack of decision making, 4) lack of mutual responsibility for meeting commitments, 5) lack of orientation towards collective results.

- **TH8: Excess of organizational democracy.** Companies that live with an excess of democracy suffer from slow decision making, which generally is because the leader is weak in that aspect, always

seeking everyone's happiness. It could also be because employees demand to be considered when making every decision.

- **TH9: Smart penny stupid dollar.** Bad habit of handling organizational finances, for which people want to save pennies when it is not needed but spend lots of dollars on irrelevant things.

- **TH10: Leaders' indecision.** The organization is stopped by the lack of decisions, generally because the leader doesn't have a concrete position, which generates low credibility and wears down employees. In many organizations leaders postpone decisions until the issue becomes an emergency.

- **TH11: Employees' dissatisfaction.** Employees who aren't satisfied with their salaries, personal or professional development, who have poor working conditions, suffer abuse from leaders, or lack purpose and workplace pride. People start to compensate for their pain or discomfort in some way, and that's why cases of robbery, lost time, organizational efforts of boycott or others can result.

- **TH12: Work silos or kingdoms.** Inability to work efficiently between areas or business units, which turn into isolated elements where there's no information transfer or collaboration among them. Each department cares only about their personal objectives, forgetting the organizational ones. This leads to a company divided, where apparently each department is the enemy of the other without considering that the real "enemy" is outside: the competition.

- **TH13: Tolerating bad habits.** Each person and organization develops bad habits through time. The problem is when these are tolerated and people learn to live with them instead of changing the situation. Many times this happens because of fear of losing something or someone in order to stop tolerating this bad habit. There can be bad results, inefficiencies, lack of fulfilled commitments, bad examples, etc. When bad habits are tolerated, particularly in leadership positions, these start to expand into the organization, because people realize that a wrong way of acting is allowed.

❯ **TH14: Toxic employees.** Are those who practice a **negative influence among working teams** not only damaging development, but also the interest and participation of each one of the collaborators? They sow frustration, discord and discomfort throughout the organization thanks to behaviors that can typically be presented as one or more of the following features: laziness, causing conflicts, incompetence, lying, stealing, arrogance, negativity, envy, etc.

❯ **TH15: High level of centralized decisions.** When the company grows, the founder starts to delegate decisions so she can work faster and more efficiently. However, despite the number of people, decisions end up in the hands of a couple of people, which makes the company slow and fragile.

❯ **TH16: High dependency on the founder.** It's when the organization can't detach from the founder or CEO. In this case, the company lives thanks to the existence, effort, and decisions of the founder, which risks the life of the company, because if he dies, then the company dies too. It is also known as "self-employment" or the Founders Trap (Ichak Adizes). There's a popular saying: "When the owner sneezes, the company gets pneumonia."

❯ **TH17: Monster with 2 or more heads.** It happens mainly when two or more founders have the same responsibilities, which provokes confusion and uncertainty, and results from an ego war where employees are in constant crossfire because of the contradictory instructions from their leaders.

❯ **TH18: "If you pay peanuts, you get monkeys".** This popular phrase explains that if you pay low salaries to your employees, you can't expect the best execution from them because this generates dissatisfaction and poor execution.

❯ **TH19: The company grew faster than its members.** This mainly happens because of the lack of development in leadership and / or technical skills, so the potential of the organization is limited.

❯ **TH20: The Scapegoat game (blaming others).** Not being held accountable means that team members are always searching for

someone to blame for their actions or results. It's also presented because of fear of the leaders' retaliations.

- ❯ **TH21: The CEO is a messenger.** It's when the leader gets involved in the conflicts between two or more members, and handles the situation separately to conciliate individually, instead of advising both parties to debate with each other to reach a fair solution.

- ❯ **TH22: Rich owner, poor company (or any combination).** This habit starts when the needs and luxuries from the owner are above the company's, which leads to scarcity or dissatisfaction. There is a series of word combinations, the previous is possibly the most common one. The optimum would be: rich company, rich owner.

- ❯ **TH23: Millenials are a problem.** This generation has different needs; however, that has become an excuse for not taking responsibility to motivate them. Each generational change brings challenges and also great benefits. The real problem of that generation is their lack of tolerance for frustration, which is seen as a problem because they haven't learned how to use it to their benefit.

- ❯ **TH24: Growing broke.** It's when a company is growing, but the profits aren't growing at the same pace and cash flow is limited. For the outside world, everything is ideal and perfect, but this is a bad position to be in because as time passes, the company has fewer resources that support healthy growth.

- ❯ **TH25: EVERYTHING is a priority!** There's a popular saying: "When everything is urgent, nothing really is." This happens because of a constant lack of focus on what really matters. Time and resources are limited, so trying to solve everything at the same time leads to doing many things in a mediocre way, instead of doing a few with excellence.

- ❯ **TH26: Meeting madness.** It's the excessive tendency of carrying out unnecessary work meetings where decisions can't be made, and because of these meetings the team can't work effectively. Work meetings are a tool that when not used correctly, can provoke confusion and time loss.

- **TH27: Go with the flow financially (Lack of budget).** There's no control over expenses and incomes; this generates a limited vision of the company and a reactive culture of ignorance of financial reality, which leads to making decisions without knowing the risk or impact that these can have.

- **TH28: Sales guide the ship.** The lack of knowledge about the ideal customer and core business makes any option of sales attractive to the company. This leads to having many priorities, little specialization, and less consistent decisions for a long-term plan. Besides, sales aren't generating profits, which makes the company's situation worse. Also, they set deadlines for deliveries which aren't met; this leads to customer dissatisfaction and a bad reputation.

- **TH29: Unclear organizational chart and structure.** The members of the organization don't understand who is responsible for what, and to whom results have to be reported.

- **TH30: Flying Blind.** The organization has no indicator boards that present their reality. Sales aren't the only indicator that generates vision; it's necessary to implement on every level of the company kpi dashboards that portray the development of activities.

- **TH31: Promote to incompetence.** Better known as "The Peter principle", it was studied and coined by Laurence J. Peter, who defines it as: when people do a good job they get promoted to positions with more responsibilities, until they reach a position where they can't fulfill the objectives of their job and reach the highest level of incompetence. For example, when a salesman is promoted to Sales director without having leadership skills, the result would be winning a bad leader and losing a good salesman.

- **TH32: Ostrich syndrome.** Like the ostrich that buries its head in the sand to avoid watching what scares it or that it dislikes, but even by not watching it can still be exposed to a threat. Directive teams avoid facing the reality where they live, they deny it. They pretend everything's perfect without facing the facts, limitations, and weaknesses they have.

❶ **TH33: Multiple hats.** When someone at the organization takes on multiple functions and / or roles, leading to not developing any function correctly. It happens because of lack of the right organizational structure or lack of staff.

❶ **TH34: Water cooler talk.** The lack of an official, clear, and efficient communication methods in the company that leads employees jumping to conclusions of their reality based on what they say when they talk with each other.

Dan: Wow, it's a long list, and the worst thing is that I identified many of them with what we experience at Plastypack nowadays, and others that we have experienced before. I have mixed emotions. On one hand, it's uncomfortable knowing that there are many of these toxic habits going on in the company, which made me realize that they are self-defeating for the future plans of the company. On the other hand, I feel relieved knowing I'm not the only one who's going through such things.

Rony: What are the three toxic habits you identified that are present at your company?

Dan: Well, from all of our conversations, the diagnosis you made and my perspective, I think we have more than three, but those that have more impact are: Scapegoat, CEO as messenger, flying blind, high dependency on the CEO, work silos and toxic employees. I know you only asked for three, but I think those six explain much of our reality as a company.

Rony: Can you give me an example?

Dan: The day I met you I told you about the two directors who don't get along, Carlos and Victor. They don't know how to collaborate or work together. They don't like each other and their personalities aren't compatible; and since they can't solve their differences, they use me as a messenger. Carlos comes to me and asks for my help when he needs to ask Victor to do something, so I have to ask him. It has become a vicious cycle of being their messenger, which frustrates me a lot, not

only because it's not effective, but because I have a million things to do and I can't be playing ping pong, but above all, it's wearing me down, it seems like I'm working with children and not professionals. Oh! Only saying it out loud angers me. About toxic employees, there are people at the company that I know aren't right for their positions, some of them for their bad results and others for having a bad attitude. Nevertheless, I need them for the daily operations. At least once a week I receive a complaint in my office about some of these people I'm identifying as toxic employees. I hadn't yet made any decision because I didn't realize it was a problem letting them stay at the company, but now it's clearer to me, I can see the damage they can do. And now, thinking out loud, I think the toxic habit that has more impact is "Scapegoat, the game of blaming others", which if I understood correctly, goes by the name of "excusitis."

Rony: Yes, these last two are like brothers, very similar situations. Both cases consist of avoiding responsibility, in the blame game, blaming someone else for your mistakes, and in "excusitis," justifying yourself and making excuses.

Dan: Well, these two toxic habits are driving me crazy. On some occasions I lose self-control and start yelling at everyone when employees make excuses. They give me every reason why things CAN'T be done when I'm paying them to tell me things CAN be done. I want to have a cultural environment where I can trust my team, that what they promise, they fulfill. I want to deal with professionals. This is a company, not a kindergarten.

Dan stopped talking and started breathing because as he explained things he got more and more angry. He sat in a chair, placed his feet on the floor and started to breathe slowly. This was a technique that he learned at a course of meditation and stress management. Once he was ready, he inhaled deeply for the last time and while exhaling he opened his eyes and said:

Dan: How can we solve this?

Rony: With the tools and methodologies we are implementing. It's important for you to be patient. A change of culture doesn't happen

overnight, it's little by little; we'll make evaluations, decisions, and put them into action, measuring results and starting a new cycle.

Dan: So this is trial and error?

Rony: The tools we use are effective, but the results of the implementation of the decisions you make with your team can't be predicted. At this moment, the fact that you're conscious of what you are experiencing with these toxic habits will be an eye opener to things you should no longer tolerate, and to different actions you should start taking.

Dan: For starters, I will definitely not accept any more excuses nor be used as a messenger. How can I do that?

Rony: With kpi dashboards and effective meetings. We'll do a detailed review of the tools and how to implement them. It's important that you know there will be a time in the process of change where you'll wake up, feel frustrated and probably want to give up because problems and conflicts that "didn't exist" will start to rise at the company, especially with the leadership team. The reality is that they already exist, but people find different ways to deal with them. The process will provide the right tools to generate a healthy conflict between all parties, oriented towards the same goals.

Dan: I understand. I suppose doing things differently will take us out of our comfort zone, but as I mentioned some weeks ago, this can't go on. I understand the warning you're giving me. I'll be supervising and will have more patience, considering that the long-term objectives that I seek to achieve through this coaching process is scaling the company, ensuring its continuity, and getting my freedom back.

Rony: Perfect. In the meantime, we'll see each other in three weeks. I'll send you the data of where we'll be meeting.

Conclusions:

⦿ You should understand in which organizational stage you are and acknowledge the toxic habits in order to replace them with more adequate habits.

⦿ Habits are generated by the members of the leadership team, so the key is to shape a leadership team that knows how to operate together, that will free the CEO of many decisions and responsibilities.

5 BUILDING A COLLABORATION TEAM.

> ❱ If you don't think you're part of the problem, you aren't part of the solution either. That's the key to collaboration.
>
> ❱ To achieve having a company where not everything depends on you, you should be a team leader; each member should be responsible for the roles, decisions and results related to their function.

Dan has been working tirelessly to carry his organization forward, but everything has to go through his hands so he can't be absent even for a couple of days because any day-to-day operation can become an emergency, like payroll, production planning, following up on overdue customers, etc. This turns his company into a self-employment enterprise. Maybe a very well-paid self-employment but with high costs, many sleepless nights, high commitments, fewer vacations and a self-abusive boss, to the point where employees can easily go on vacations but not him.

We met at the beach, where I knew there would be an Army command practice. They usually work out at that beach the third Wednesday of each month at 7 a.m. Dan arrived punctually, with two coffees in his hands and a look of curiosity on his face.

Dan: I'm intrigued, what are we doing at the beach at 7 a.m.? Are we going to take the day off and enjoy the beach?

Rony: That would be fun, but that's not the reason why I asked you to meet me here. You see, the pillar that will help us fulfill the vision

you have in mind is the people surrounding you. The leadership team is the key that will make everything either function or disappear.

Dan: Ok, and what does the beach have to do with the problems of my company?

Rony: In a few minutes, you'll see a group of soldiers running from the north. They belong to a special command and work out at this beach every now and then.

Dan: And what do they have to do with my company?

Rony: They don't, but what you are about to see does. The Army has dominated the art of building teams and making them work coordinated. The members trust one another and work for the same objective.

Dan: I can see them coming, there are even more than I thought. But they're crazy, they are running in the water. I thought they would be running on the sand.

Rony: On the sand? That's a child's game; they are at another level. The exercise they're doing is called 40x40x40. They run 40 kilometers, at 40 cm of water depth and with 40 kilos on their backs. They want to improve on the time they achieved the last time, and nobody can be left behind.

Dan: Nobody? And what happens if one of them has an accident or simply doesn't feel like running?

Rony: The others will encourage him, carry his weight and if necessary, carry him too. But nobody can be left behind. Do you think that if by any chance they were in enemy territory and one of them was exhausted, do you think they would say, "Rest a little, see you in a bit; we'll be waiting for you to catch up on us?" No way! The group's strength can be observed by their weakest member. They can't let the weakest make them vulnerable.

Dan: Yes, I have heard the phrase "You are as strong as the weakest link." I think I didn't understand it until now.

Rony: And wait to see them approach and make the last challenge.

Dan: What? After that madness of exercise 40x40x40 they still do another challenge?

Rony: Indeed, they lift a log of about 250 pounds..

Dan: I can see that they are divided into groups of eight.

Rony: This exercise will force them and teach them to work as a team; as well as from other skills like being a leader or a follower.

Dan: See how the first group is having trouble organizing, and in the second group there's a member who looks exhausted. I don't think he could help them lift the log.

Rony: To increase complexity, they should lift the log simultaneously, because if not, some of them might be worn out and even have an accident. What else do you see?

Dan: I see that the team with an exhausted member has to make an extra effort.

Rony: That's called **compensating**. The load of the member that's not carrying the same weight as the others is compensated by the other seven. Because the log doesn't discriminate nor does it have compassionate understanding that there's one member less. The log still weighs the same no matter who helps and who doesn't.

Dan: The other group is struggling a little to decide who gives the instructions. They're not coordinating and the process seems painful.

Rony: What would you call that situation?

Dan: Poor leadership.

Rony: Could also be "poor followers". One has to know how to be a leader, but also have the humility of not carrying it out when it's not needed. Look how the red-headed kid doesn't agree with the one who's trying to lead the group. There's a little ego battle going on, which is making the entire team struggle. In the US Army there's a phrase taught to the troops that says "lead, follow or get out of the way." Teamwork is very difficult to achieve, to the point where not even finances nor strategy weigh more than developing organizations. Patrick Lencioni says that "if you can get every member of the organization to row in the same direction, you'll be able to dominate any industry in any market, against any competition at any time."

Dan: I agree. It's very hard to build a team. Between the ego wars and cultural or personal differences, it's an art.

Rony: Yes, human beings are imperfect, selfish and tend to misread things, which makes groups dysfunctional.

Dan: I get why you brought me here. Those kinds of things happen at my company. The deficiency that some members of the company have is compensated by the others because they are trying to reach a certain volume of sales and production. I feel I have so many useless people at the company.

Rony: How many useless people do you have in the organization who don't add value?

Dan: I'm not sure, but there are some.

Rony: Going deeper, is there anyone that is still at the company because you feel responsible for keeping them despite knowing that they don't collaborate correctly? Do the others have to compensate for the log's weight of 250 pounds?

Dan: Yes, I have a couple in mind. Mainly people who have been there from the beginning, and I would feel very responsible and guilty if I let them go.

Rony: So, is it better to keep them at the company?

Dan: No, but I don't know what to do.

Rony: Unfortunately, organizations grow faster than their members. Some members don't care about escalating personally and professionally, so they become a burden for the company. Sometimes we have to let them go, for their sake and the company's.

Dan: Why for their sake? Letting them go will be bad for them. They won't have a job or income.

Rony: In the short term you are right. They won't have income. But what you don't see is that when people are in an environment where they don't feel they can contribute, they feel useless and without a purpose; it destroys their self-esteem. On one occasion while working with a client, we made an analysis of the people who worked there, their contribution to the group and if they fitted with the organization's culture. It was

called top grading analysis, a tool that I'll teach you how to use later. We discovered there was an employee that had been working since the company began, but at the moment of the evaluation, David, the CEO, who you've met already, discovered that Joyce, the employee I just mentioned, was a type C, which he had known for a couple years, and for that he should have terminated their work relationship, or as some would say: "free her future".

Dan: That sounds very cruel.

Rony: Wait and see why it was more cruel to keep her at the company. She didn't deliver good results, so the rest of her colleagues had to compensate for her deficiency to achieve the objectives of that division. Besides, she had some habits and behaviors that bothered her colleagues. For example, the last Friday of the month David would order pizzas for everyone at the company, and Joyce took containers to take some to her house. Sometimes there were people who didn't get any because of the pieces she was taking home. Later, it was discovered that she also took toilet paper to her house.

Dan: Poor lady, maybe she had an important financial problem at her house.

Rony: That doesn't make any difference. Stealing is stealing. It's breaking the trust of the people you work with. And actually, she wasn't taking the pizza and toilet paper because she needed it, but because of revenge. It was a way of demonstrating the frustration and anger she had with the company. When we concluded that she was a type C employee and that there should be a decent exit plan for her, David couldn't make the decision. His heart was breaking. She was 40 years old. You have to know that two years before David already knew she wasn't a good employee, so ever since she was 38 years old he could've taken her destiny in his hands. It took David two more years to make the decision, and when he did, things were very bad. She was sabotaging the company, her colleagues hated her, and David avoided her. The point is that it is not the same for a 38-year-old person to search for a new job, with good self-esteem, than for a 42-year-old with her self-esteem destroyed.

Dan: Now that I have the complete picture, I get your point. It would have been better to let her go as soon as David realized she was a type C employee, or as you said: "free her future" for her sake and the company's as well.

Rony: Joyce didn't grow at the same speed as the company, and David, didn't help her grow or leave, which provoked a series of anomalies and dysfunctions at the company. As CEO you have to worry about people growing at the same speed as the company, and when they do not fit due to cultural or performance factors, it's time to let that person go. All CEOs I know have their "Joyce," someone who was once loyal at the beginning, but the company grew and she didn't.

Dan: I think in my case it would be Elias.

Rony: It's good you can identify someone! I would take note to talk about Elias later. So, going back to the exercise of the soldiers that we're watching, we should make sure we have a team that supports each other and works for a common good, that knows how to work together, that sees that when a member of the group needs help, they provide it. Having more people than the organization can handle or needs eventually becomes a problem. The RPE indicator, which in your case is $38k USD per employee, indicates that you have more people than you need, or that your sales are low. Having more people generates a more negative effect than expected, more conflict and inefficiency. Since there's more people, employees tend to relax and there could be more compensation of workloads, but not necessarily more efficiency.

Dan: And what can I do?

Rony: First I would like you to understand the big picture, and you can make decisions later. Let's continue. For you to achieve greater results so that the organization can depend less on you, we need to **build a leadership team that is solid**, that works towards a common objective, and that supports each other to achieve the results of the company. Did you have an opportunity to think about who you want to be part of your leadership team?

Dan: Yes, we'll call them directors, but really they're not, and they don't have the salary for that position.

Rony: That's perfect. We already talked about that. I just have to confirm how your leadership team will be shaped because we'll have our first meeting with them soon.

Dan: Carlos in Sales; Victor in Operations; Diana in Human Resources; and Alex in Administration and Finances.

Rony: So if we draw your org chart it would be like this:

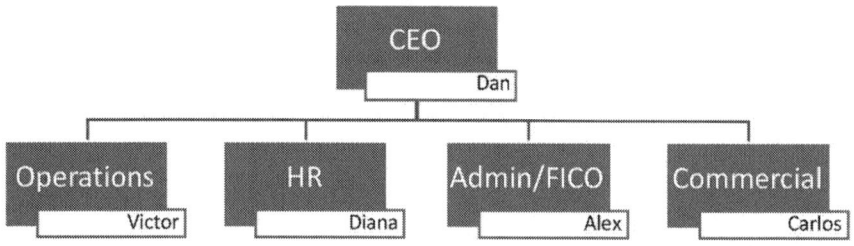

Dan: I have my doubts about Diana and Alex because they are at a lower level compared with the others. They have less experience; besides, they avoid saying what they think, they're more introverted and even shy.

Rony: We'll get to that; they will align. It's only a matter of providing them the right environment and tools. Will this team tell you things as they are?

Dan: I hope so. I'm not an expert on every area, I prefer that they advise me on what to do in their departments.

Rony: That's called "don't be the smartest brain in the room." Congrats! It's a very mature way of thinking, because if you had all the answers and knew more about their area than them, probably you'd be surrounded by the wrong people. Now that the structure is clear, there are two critical questions you should answer so that you and each one of them know for sure what each one is responsible for and how success can be measured. **What's the fundamental purpose of their positions and how do you measure success?**

Dan: What do you mean by the fundamental purpose of their positions? I need people who solve things.

Rony: Of course, but what do you specifically want them to solve? Let's use Carlos the sales director as an example. What's the fundamental purpose of his position at your company?

Dan: To sell. The fundamental purpose is to sell. It seems like common sense to me, don't you think?

Rony: The truth is that common sense is the least common of all senses. Common sense is a criterion for making decisions, and the way you make them isn't the same way they do.

Dan: You can't imagine how that frustrates me. Multiple times I have hoped people would use their common sense and answer correctly, as I would like.

Rony: But you haven't taught them to think and answer the way you'd like. That's why, instead of abiding by their "common sense" you should be clear about what you expect from each person. So, if we sharpen the aim of commercial management, we could say that its fundamental purpose is to increase the revenue of the company. Selling is the means to an end, a task. From my perspective, the sales director should provide a higher revenue to the company, and sales are just a way of doing it.

Dan: True. The reason why I want a sales director is to generate higher revenue, and sales is only one way. There's also other options such: donations, raising capital, getting more investors, among other things.

Rony: Exactly. How would you measure the success of that position? Meaning, what would be the indicator?

Dan: That's an easy one: income in the bank account. It's more important for me to know how much money enters the bank account than knowing how many quotations I've made. Which are also important, but quotations are a means to an end. I'm interested in knowing the end.

Rony: I love it, I can see how fast you're absorbing the methodology.

We continued working with the rest of the positions for a few more moments until we decided the fundamental purpose and success indicators for each position.

Dan: Ok, summing up: Operations, its fundamental purpose is customer satisfaction, and the success indicator is delivering on time and correctly; Administration, its fundamental purpose is optimizing resources and the success indicator would be cash flow, which gives us life and helps us support our growth; for Human Resources, I think the fundamental purpose is customer satisfaction and the success indicator would be ENPS (employee net promoter score). For me, as CEO, my fundamental purpose is to grow the organization and my success indicator is the company's increase of value and set the level of the organization's dependency on the leader.

Rony: Great! Now that we have the org chart and the fundamental purposes and indicators are clear, it's time for us to meet with your team, to have a strategic meeting where you can explain to them the vision you have, the organizational structure and the elements that will help people work as a team. We need an organizational culture where the person who has the role and accountability can also be empowered to make decisions, because if he doesn't have that, he avoids the consequences. Have you ever heard someone from your team saying: "Yes, I'm specialized in maintenance, but you don't let me make decisions. Why did you hire me"?

Dan: No, no one has ever said that to me, but that happened to me at my previous job, where I felt very frustrated with my boss, who didn't let me make decisions about my responsibilities.

Rony: Maybe no one has ever told you that, but that doesn't mean it's not happening. Let's make sure that responsibilities come by the hand of empowerment. At the end, each one of them is responsible for the results they achieve at their departments they lead.

Dan: Yes, definitely. We need to build a solid leadership team, which I can rely on to make decisions and execute plans, which has my back and vice versa.

Rony: I'm glad you're starting to find solutions. They will free you. Now, we need to schedule a meeting with your team.

Dan: Are we also meeting here at the beach to watch the soldiers exercising?

Rony: No, but you can tell them the experience you had watching them. Actually, we should meet in a meeting room, where we can talk without interruptions and where people can openly communicate. Preferably, outside the office.

Dan: How about next Thursday at a meeting room that I'm renting from some shared offices in the South of the city?

Rony: That's perfect, I'll meet you there.

Dan: Before you go, could you tell me what's the ideal number of people to build a leadership team?

Rony: According to Jeff Bezos, from an Amazon study of team management, it's the number of people you can feed with two large pizzas.

Dan: Ha ha ha, really? Two pizzas?

Rony: Yes, the study says the ideal number to build a leadership team is about six people.

Dan: And what if someone eats a lot? Would we have fewer members? Ha ha ha, we both laughed.

Rony: Actually, there's a lot of science behind the number of people a leader should handle directly. **The more people, the more dispersed their attention is, and relationships are more complex.** Jeff Bezos says that teams that communicate a lot are dysfunctional, and adds: "We should be trying to figure out ways for teams to communicate less with each other, not more."

It makes sense. Effective communication is direct and simple. The reasoning behind this is quite simple: more people = more everything: more coordination, more bureaucracy, more chaos, basically more of everything that can slow things down. Individual performance suffers and people are less committed.

Dan: So, the more people on the team the more problems we're going to have?

Rony: As the Harvard psychologist and group dynamic expert J. Richard Hackman pointed out in his article HBR (https://hbr.org/2009/05/why-teams-dont-work): "The larger the group, the more process problems the members will have to carry out their collective work. [...] It's the management of links between members which causes team problems". Look at this formula that shows how links grow exponentially:

$$\text{\# of connections} = \frac{n(n-1)}{2}$$

n = # of members in a team

That means that a small Start-up with three people has three links to maintain. If we double the size of this team, it would grow five times the number of links to 15. A larger team of 12 members has to worry about 66 connections. And for a group of 50, the number of connections scales to 1225.

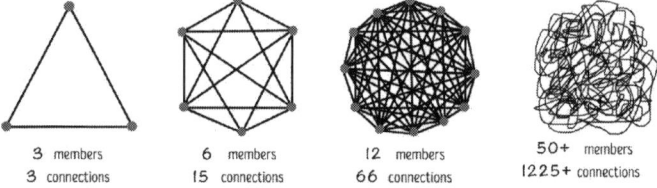

| 3 members | 6 members | 12 members | 50+ members |
| 3 connections | 15 connections | 66 connections | 1225+ connections |

Dan: So, the more links I have, the bigger the risk of bad administration, bad interpretation and bad communication. The time and effort needed to keep everyone on the same page becomes a snowball. Is there some software that can help me handle the tasks of my staff?

Rony: Yes, there is some: Monday.com, Trello and Asana. However, there's a simple tool that I'll show you later, named: **Action plan.**

Dan: Perfect, so see you next week then.

A week later, the staff arrived on time at the meeting room with a nervous look in their eyes, because they didn't know what was going to happen. This was the first time they were asked to meet outside the office. Dan welcomed the group.

Dan: Good morning everyone. Thanks for arriving on time. I know some of you are nervous and curious about this meeting. The reason we're here is because I want to make the company grow without everything depending on me. I want to have control over the company and achieve that the dog wags the tail and not the other way around. That said, I need the help of each and every one of you to have a better company, with better results, happy people and also, so that we can decentralize the decisions that rely on me today. You are my leadership team, and Rony is here to help us fulfill objectives and also work as a team. I think everyone had the opportunity to meet him during your interviews.

While showing them an image on the screen I asked:

Rony: If a team is secured by the waist while scaling a mountain in the Himalaya, who sets the speed of the team?

Carlos says that it's the one at the front, Alex the one at the back, Dan the fattest one; we all laughed. I replied:

Rony: Actually, the speed is set by the slowest member of the team. I don't know if he is at the front, back, or in the middle, if he is fat or thin; but he is definitely the slowest member. We should pay attention to realize who the slowest member of our team is, to help him lighten his load, motivate him, or do something else that helps the team move forward. At some point, all of us may be the slowest member: how good are you at asking for help? Getting help? Providing help?

Victor: Actually, everyone here is too proud to demonstrate weaknesses or ask for help.

Diana: If I ask for help, I think that I'll be misjudged as someone who doesn't contribute to the team.

Rony: It's normal to feel like that. Unfortunately, we're taught to be strong and not show weaknesses or vulnerabilities. But do you realize that people who ask for help are the strongest?

Carlos: Yes, I have an uncle that's very authentic. He doesn't pretend to be someone else or perfect. He openly says he's not very good at math and that he hires people who are specialized in finances and administration to help him at his company, which makes him very successful and efficient.

Rony: A few years ago I met a man who had a very successful company. His revenue was high and he was happy. I asked for his recipe of success and he said "I'm illiterate." When he saw my look of surprise he approached me and said: "I can solve the problem of not knowing how to read or write by hiring people who do, people whom I can trust completely to the point of asking them to sign a contract that I can't read." As you can see, we've been taught wrong. Asking for help is the key to success. We should also have the humility to get and provide it. At this moment Dan's asking for your help to achieve this organizational change. Who's on board?

ME, everyone replied.

Rony: Great. Then we're on the right path. One of the most important things to help this company grow is to have a good leadership team that leads the organization towards success. According to Dan, he has already shown you the GPS; point A, where we are today, and point B, towards where we're going.

Dan: Yes, I already showed it to them. Is there something else you would like to know about it?

Victor: I think it's clear. What I don't know is how are we going to achieve that.

Alex: I believe that's why we're here.

Rony: Indeed. We're going to introduce another element that will help us. Have you ever heard the term "common good?" What does it mean to you?

Diana: Is the idea of something beneficial for everyone.

Carlos: I think it is not for everyone but for most people.

Rony: I couldn't have explained it better. I agree with Carlos's definition, it's what's good for most people and should be well oriented. The following question helps companies align towards "common good": what's better for the company?

Alex: How will asking that question help a company's staff?

Dan: I think it will help us change our behavior and decision making. For example, last week, were the decisions you made about the payment plan based on what was better for Plastypack or for you and your team?

Carlos: Before you answer, Alex, I think your decision was selfish because you solved a problem at your department, but in the commercial and operational team we had many problems. Your decision placed us in a vulnerable situation.

Alex: I promise my decision wasn't badly intended. I thought I was doing the right thing.

Rony: I believe you, but now we are learning to think and act as a team. It's not about crucifying yourself in the process, I think Dan was

only giving an example. You should have many examples where each one of you has made decisions selfishly. As I said, that's normal, because that's the way we were taught, but we can control our minds and our lives. That way of thinking only divides people. The competition is not outside the company, it's inside. I don't think we should worry about what the competition can do in your industry. Right now the problem is that the team is stumbling over itself.

Carlos: We can't lose sight of the competition. They are taking over the market completely.

Dan: I understand what Rony's saying. We can't lose sight of the competition but right now, and probably for the following months, we should improve our way of working, build a team where we can collaborate, and strengthen the company so that the competition fears us. At this moment, they're only laughing at our mistakes. The customers know that we're screwed, that we are not a collaborative team.

Rony: A great example of **collaboration** is Las Vegas. Each hotel worries about serving their customers and about having a high occupancy, which means: filling the hotels with as many people as possible. But Las Vegas is well organized. They understand their biggest competition is outside Las Vegas: any other tourist destination, so hotels promote services of other hotels, something that only happens there. You can easily go from one hotel to the other, watch advertisements of the Zumanity show which is from the New York New York hotel at the Caesars Palace hotel. What I'm trying to say here is that hotels from Las Vegas seek common good. They ask themselves "what's better for Las Vegas?", so they make sure that tourists can have a more complete experience from Las Vegas than only from the Bellagio hotel for example, because when you travel to Las Vegas you want to experience all the emotions that this destination generates, including every hotel, show and casino.

Dan: I just remembered the story of the crab buckets; there's a bucket of European crabs that costs $32 per kilo and has a lid, and another bucket of Latin American crabs that costs $15 per kilo and has

no lid. European crabs help each other get out, and that's why their bucket has a lid. The Latino bucket of crabs has no lid because when a crab tries to get out, the others drag it to the bottom.

Rony: That's right. That metaphor explains correctly the Las Vegas hotels phenomenon, as well as the philosophy which functional teams work with, which consists of helping each other and thinking what's best for the company. An example of this philosophy is being carried out is at the National Football League, where each one of the 32 teams is independent and makes its own decisions, as long as these decisions won't affect the NFL franchise. They all understand that they're part of something greater; each team contributes to the league, and if one team disappears, the entire league gets in trouble because of the logistics and the revenue problems it generates. The sum of strength from each team is what makes the NFL so powerful. But this doesn't only remain in words, it actually makes an impact on their personal finances. They have an agreement called supplemental revenue-sharing pool. Everyone contributes with a percentage of their revenue, and it's equally distributed among every team.

Diana: And what does the NFL gain by doing that?

Rony: That the weakest teams of the league will always be alive, and also the wellbeing of the NFL.

Dan: I like the idea, I love the philosophy of thinking we are all working together in the same company, where we seek the common good and care about Plastypack's interests. It will also help me change my decision making, because now I realize I was not making decisions based on common good. I remember a conversation I had with Rony about the fact that I'm not getting a competitive salary for my position or milking the company's profit as you say, and that is bad for the company. I thought it was better if I didn't get a salary so we can have cash flow, but now I understand I'm damaging the company by NOT getting a CEO salary, and above all, damaging its road to the future. If I was getting a competitive salary and for any reason we want to bring in a new CEO to replace me, the organization will be used to paying that salary.

Alex: That will help me have better control over the budget, because as we do it today it is difficult to handle and very unpredictable. Some weeks you withdraw a little bit of money, other weeks a larger one, and sometimes nothing at all. To be honest, that's very difficult for me. I'm glad that's changing.

Diana: Why did you mention a new CEO for the company? Are you sick? Is something wrong? Does anyone know something I don't?

Dan: Calm down Diana, everything's fine. This idea came from a series of conversations I had with Rony that made me realize there are people who can execute the CEO role better than me, and possibly for less money, besides the fact that I enjoy creating new products and being in touch with customers rather than directing a company. We need this replacement.

Rony: That's a very mature decision. If you do what you like you'll have better results. Today we don't have the resources or someone in our spotlight, but that will happen eventually. Dan, could you show the team the organizational chart including the fundamental purpose and success indicators?

For about an hour, the team was calmly exchanging, discussing, and clarifying different ideas from the organizational structure and the fundamental purpose proposals. With everyone's help, they made a small change to take responsibilities from Victor, development of new projects, as well as maintenance. Both were distracting him from his main task, and these responsibilities were passed temporarily to Dan, the Development director, because in the future he is either going to be replaced by another CEO or with someone who takes the "new" position of Development, or this position is going to be eliminated, redistributing his functions. Sometimes two positions are covered by the same person. In those cases their name is marked with quotation marks to know that he has a secondary function that should be replaced ASAP.

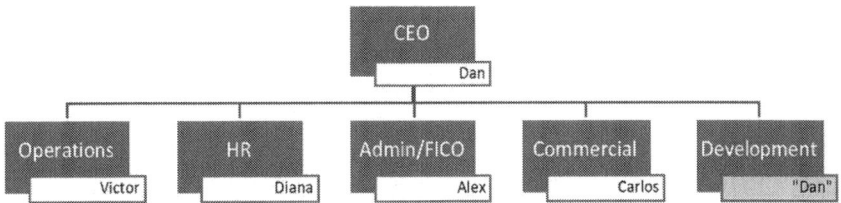

Rony: I would like to know how you are feeling with the structure and responsibility definitions.

Alex: To be honest, much better. It seems like the functions are clearer. I know now what Dan and the organization expect from me.

Diana: As for me, I have mixed emotions. I feel relieved and also under pressure. Relieved, because finally I know what to focus on and which indicator measures my development. Under pressure because now I know that having a measurable objective will demand better results.

Rony: **The organizational structure or organizational chart is a "living document,"** meaning it should be adapted through time to reflect reality or to restructure the company to achieve results.

Dan: What do you mean by living document?

Rony: It's very common that companies have a non-updated organizational chart. This document should be checked every quarter and updated if needed, to ensure flexibility, objective fulfillment according to a strategic plan, and to keep all members up to date.

Diana: I like that. The name of every member of the company should be on that organizational chart and everyone should know to whom they should report, what's expected from them, and how the success of his job is measured, even the newest members. When I started working at the company, they showed me an organizational chart with names of people who were no longer at the company. I believe the organizational chart should be updated each time we welcome a new member and the document should be shared with the entire staff, so that we all can know who does what and to whom each member has to report.

Rony: Let's continue going deeper and changing our way of thinking. In the organizational chart you made, I'm going to draw a blue circle circling Victor with the rest of you and a red circle with Victor and the people working beneath him. To which Team does Victor belong?

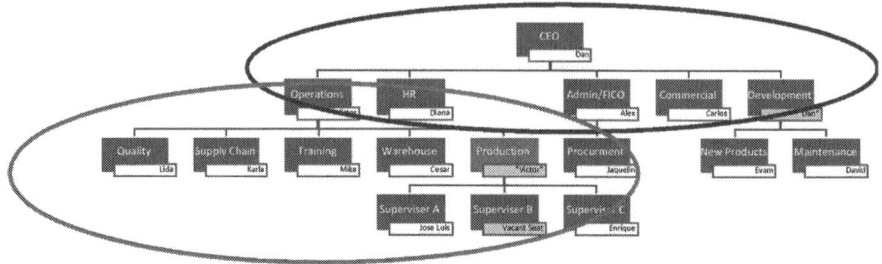

Victor: I would say to both of them.

Alex: To the red one, but I think that also to the blue one. Mainly, to the red one because those are the people he works with every day, and thanks to them he achieves his results.

Dan: To the blue one. Because he should have more commitment with me.

Carlos: Obviously to the red one, without them he couldn't achieve his goals.

Rony: I know it's a tough question, but very valuable to understand because to misinterpret it can cause many problems or create toxic habits for the company. Victor "belongs to" the blue team and "leads" the red team.

It may seem like the same thing, but that little difference makes a big change in his way of thinking and behaving. The key is to know you should always think first about what's better for the company. If I belong to the blue team I should think about the sake of the company, but if I belong to the red one, I should think about personal or particular interests of the department. I'll give an example that happens frequently in many families to explain the concept better. Some parents are discussing if their kid can go to a friend's house. The father isn't comfortable with the kid going because he feels the friend

and the environment where he lives are a bad influence for his kid. The mother doesn't want to limit the circle of friends of her kid, because the kid doesn't have many friends. After privately discussing this, they reach an agreement and decide the kid CAN'T go to the friend's house. The mother approaches her kid to deliver the bad news: "Sammy, I'm sorry to tell you that you can't go to your friend's house. I want you to know I wanted you to go and defended you, but after talking to your father, we decided you can't go." Can you notice what's happening here?

Dan: Yes, the mother didn't care for the family interests, she wanted to be the "good cop" for her kid and embarrassed the father. She didn't show unity.

Rony: Exactly. The lack of unity was evident and with time it can grow, to the point where the kid can manipulate the parents to achieve what he wants. Something similar happens with employees. If they know the leadership or blue team is divided, they can and will abuse trust and take advantage of the conflict generated with the blue team. If each one of the members embraces the leadership or red team as their own and cares for its interests, a reign organization will be created, where each department has a king who rules, but forgets they belong to an empire.

Dan: I've felt some of the effects you mention at the company. I find it hard to explain to the team that we are one. At first, it seems like they bought the idea, but at daily operations they fight with the other departments as if they belong to a different company, this weakens the company.

Rony: A common way of calling these reigns is "silos." Unfortunately, working for silos is very common and a bad habit we have to eliminate.

Victor: At the previous company where I worked the divisions of departments were very evident, to the point where people started boycotts to provoke bad results in the Control area, for the purpose of making the manager get fired without anyone realizing we were attacking each other and damaging the company. These situations happened a lot, and that's why I quit. The environment became hostile: I wish those were reigns; in our case they were like gangs. You had to be

smart enough to know who you should hang out with. It seems trivial but that's the situation that I lived in, and it was horrible.

Carlos: I can identify a lot with the example of the parents. That's what my parents used to do. It took them a lot of time to make a decision, and when they did, they generally ended up angry at each other, and also with my siblings. So we learned who was going to give us more permissions depending on the subject, for social matters to my dad, and for matters of money to my mom; we manipulated our parents to get to where we wanted.

Rony: Are there people at the company who are taking advantage of their divisions or of any unhealthy conflicts to achieve personal objectives?

Diana: Definitely, there are some people on Victor's staff who know Dan is more flexible with salary increases, while Victor is stricter. That's why when they want to ask for a raise they go straight to Dan, and that has brought us many problems.

Dan: Really? That has brought problems? Sorry. It's very hard for me to say no to people who ask me for a salary increase.

Alex: But you could redirect them to the right person so that employee can make the right decision, with Diana from HR or Victor, who is their boss. I don't know about social matters, but about finance and administration, the fact of not having the right order or process for salary increases is problematic.

Diana: There is a process, but no one respects it.

Carlos: Are you blaming me again for having to increase the salary of two of my salesmen?

The tone started to rise and people wanted to argue.

Rony: Apparently, we've reached a sensitive part, a fracture of this team. I don't care if we solve the problem of salary increases today, but this team is not a team, and I realized that thanks to how you just reacted: arguing and raising your voices for small things. Now it's clearer to me why it's so difficult to achieve results as a group.

Dan: That's what I was talking about. Everyone is very sensitive and fights for things that aren't important. You keep many resentments. But I guess that's why we're here.

Rony: Right. The fact that you have different opinions is good for the team. Fighting isn't. Is anyone familiar with Patrick Lencioni's methodology of team development? Or with his book *The 5 dysfunctions of a team*?

Alex: I once heard a lecture by Patrick about dysfunction and the only thing I remember is that trust is fundamental for team building.

Rony: We're on the right path. Now I'll explain the complete model. Does anyone know something else?

Carlos: I read that book years ago. It seemed like a very interesting fable. At that time I read it with the team that I was working with. It helped us solve many differences that we had, placed things in perspective and gave us the right language. I don't remember many details, but I do remember that after we read it we could have more productive meetings with a healthy debate and people weren't offended. Moreover, we called this debate conflict.

Rony: Great! We have some knowledge in the group, and that will make things easier. I'll explain Patrick's philosophy and methodology in a very simple way: He says that every team has five levels of dysfunctions depending on how you look. He draws these levels in a pyramid.

The first dysfunction is the absence of trust between team members. This arises from their lack of willingness to be vulnerable. The members of the team that aren't willing to open up before others to accept their mistakes and weaknesses make it impossible to build trust foundations. They don't ask for or get help. Respect and trust are the basis of any community. It doesn't matter how many rules or systems there are, if you have people who you don't trust working with you, they'll eventually break the system and steal from you. Make sure you have people you trust at your company, and that they also trust each other.

Failing at building trust is harmful because it brings **the second dysfunction: fear of conflict.** Teams that have trust issues are incapable

of passionately participating in discussions. They would rather have careful conversations and an artificial harmony. What's your definition of conflict?

Alex: Conflict is to fight, to have problems or a battle.

Rony: Let me clarify the concept of **"conflict"** in a most effective way for everyone, which will strengthen the methodology. *Conflict is to have a healthy debate to find a new truth*; meaning, if you don't agree with my ideas and tell me your perspective about them, that's a conflict. We should have healthy conflict that promotes discussing our ideas in order to improve them.

Dan: I don't agree with you (said sarcastically).

Ha ha ha, everyone laughed and the environment felt more relaxed.

Rony: Ok, going back to the pyramid, the lack of conflict is a problem because **it gives strength to the third dysfunction: lack of commitment.** Only on rare occasions, without an open debate, team members truly accept decisions and commit to them; even when they pretend to agree at work meetings.

Due to this lack of commitment and acceptance, team members develop **the fourth dysfunction, which is to avoid accountability.** Without committing to a clear action plan, even the most centered and enthusiastic person tends to hesitate when telling off their colleagues for actions or conducts they do or have that are inadequate for the team.

The inability to take responsibility or accountability from both parts creates an environment where **the fifth dysfunction can thrive: lack of attention to results,** which happens when members of the team put their individual needs (like ego, development of personal career, acknowledgment) or even the needs of their departments above collective goals of the team.

Diana: I'm starting to see how we can reflect in each one of the levels. Not completely, but I can sense some behaviors we have.

Dan: I feel that what the company needs the most is people who take responsibility for their actions, decisions, and results. I think everyone is committed, but what we are failing to do is take responsibility for our

commitments. Do you know how many things people commit to me every day? It's impossible to follow everything up. The truth is I give the follow up whenever I remember and generally, when it becomes an emergency: like a customer complaint or a bigger problem. But I can't keep chasing everyone. I trust that I have professional people working in my company who can keep their word and don't need a babysitter that chases them to comply with their commitments.

Rony: This can be solved with the methodology. I don't think any of you "play dumb" intentionally. It's probably because you handle many things and commitments that make you forget about other things. On day-to-day operations, constant urgencies make people forget about the commitments they made. I'm going to show you one of the most powerful tools in the process of organizational change and growth, it's named: "action plan," which consists of three simple questions: who, what, when. From now on, I'm going to ask you to write down in the action plan any commitment that can come up when you have meetings with your team or with Dan, with your name (who), the description of the commitment (what) and the date when it will be fulfilled (when).

Dan: But that will be a long list.

Rony: It's better to have a long list than commitments that aren't fulfilled, right?

Dan: And should I check that list every day?

Rony: No, that list will be updated according to new agreements you make, but you'll check the list once a week and follow up on the expired tasks. I assure you that if the team knows you're confronting them with their commitments once a week, they'll start making an effort to meet them or stop taking them lightly.

Alex: With this pyramid of the five dysfunctions I understand what I shouldn't do, but I'm not sure I understood correctly what I should do. Could you explain that to us?

Rony: Of course. Let's take a positive focus on how a united high development team should behave.

- The basis of the pyramid is trust. Members trust one another. They know how to ask and get help.
- Conflict. All the members of the team feel they have the right capacity and openness to have constructive ideas that lead to decision debates.
- Commitment. This is where decisions should be made, that team members will respect.
- Accountability. Team members center on achieving collective results.
- Results oriented. The main focus is to get the organizational results.

Diana: I think this complements the explanation correctly, and that we should read and discuss that book as a team.

Dan: I love the idea.

Rony: To read a book every quarter as a team is a good practice for teams that want high development incorporated into their routine because it generates a common language, and at the same time, it ensures the continuity of their personal and professional development.

Ok, it's time for us to learn about an element that generates a lot of drama: decision making.

Dan: That's obvious. I always have the final say.

Everyone laughed nervously.

Rony: Tell me how's the decision making going in your work meetings?

Carlos: It isn't very common that we make decisions in our meetings. We talk endlessly without getting anywhere.

Victor: And when that happens, Dan gets exasperated and ends up imposing his decision on the team.

Dan: Of course, because we can't spend hours discussing the same thing over and over again. It drives me crazy not to move forward.

Diana: When that happens, I tend to think I'm not the right person for the company, because when we make decisions about my department and responsibilities, I don't feel I can do it by myself, which makes me question my authority at the company. I feel frustrated about not being the right person to decide specific things.

Rony: Well, I have good news for you. Once I explain the right way to make decisions it will make your jobs simpler. You'll have effective meetings and it will help strengthen your authority in the areas that are under your responsibility.

Carlos: I would pay to see that!!! If what you'll teach us will simplify our meetings you'll be my hero.

Rony: The first thing you should know, which you won't like, is that **companies aren't democratic.** It's not a place where democracy should always be present. We want the same kind of democracy we have in our country, but that cannot happen at a company.

Dan: I like what I'm hearing.

Rony: It's not always a dictatorship either. You, as CEO obviously always have the final say. But this is not about going from one end to the other. It's important that you have the ability to have a healthy debate or conflict, so you can make better decisions.

Alex: The key is to know how to make the right decisions and make fast and accurate progress.

Rony: Exactly. There are **ways to make decisions** at work meetings. These simplify decision making and give the members clear expectations to be able to proceed easily. These types of decisions are:

- **Democratic,** in that the point of view of every member is asked for and they vote. When most members have voted, they can proceed.

- **Autocratic,** in that the leader has the final say. The leader already makes the decision and communicates it to the rest of the team. He wants to know what each member will do after this decision.

- **Consensus,** where, after having a discussion, people try to get to an agreement which EVERY member is happy with.

- **Consultancy,** where the department has to consult every member to give their point of view to make a responsible decision.

- **Delegated,** which requires humility. It implies knowing you're not the best at making decisions, so you give that responsibility to someone else.

Rony: Which is the type of decisions you work with?

Alex: Mostly "autocratic" because it's Dan who makes the decisions.

Dan: I try to make you part of the discussion in the decision-making process, but I get exasperated when you don't conclude or decide something, and I impose my decision.

Diana: I feel that sometimes you are so used to being the boss that you forget to listen to us.

Carlos: I think the company has evolved. Before, Dan used to make every decision, so it was autocratic or even a dictatorship type. But for a while I've seen how Dan wants to get people involved with decision making, so in our meetings we tend to make decisions by consensus. It's almost impossible for everyone to agree and it becomes endless; so Dan feels frustrated and makes the decision autocratically. It's confusing.

Rony: When companies revolve around their owner, he's the one who makes the decisions. Especially when it's a Start-up, decisions are autocratic, or as Carlos said, a dictatorship. But when the company grows, it's impossible for the owner to make every decision, and it's hard to let go of control. Eventually, the CEO realizes that kind of decision making it's not right for the company and makes an unsuccessful attempt to do the opposite, which is making decisions by consensus. But he also realizes that the company slows down and he just stops making decisions. He feels frustrated and goes back to being autocratic with everyone but the people who have gained his trust. When the company grows, decision making has to be more flexible, to keep a valid, dynamic, active, profitable, and helpful company.

Victor: It's not easy to apply that change in our decision making. I've seen it in the evolution my brother has had at his company. He went through the same: he was a dictator and tried to be a consensus leader. Then he started reading books and material in the *Harvard Business Review,* and things improved.

Rony: From now on, I'm going to ask you that when you have to make decisions in a meeting, the member of the team who is accountable for it has to say how he intends to make the decision at

the end of the discussion or debate. That way it's going to be clearer for the rest of the team how they're going to proceed, and decision making will be simpler and evident. There's no magic formula that indicates which type of decision making should be used most of the time. Every situation is different and the company has to maintain its flexibility.

Dan: It's like having a Swiss Army knife that has many tools and I decide which one to use according to the situation. I don't always need to use the knife or scissors. That's why it has many tools.

Rony: Exactly, like a Swiss knife. You now have five different ways of making decisions. You have to decide together which one you'll use in each situation. Now that everyone's clear about how to make things more flexible and effective as a team, let's do the first exercise: you have to identify three main strengths that can lead this group to success to ensure a growth plan, and the three most dangerous weaknesses that can sabotage that plan.

The team had the chance to put into practice what they learned by having an honest discussion about what's working and not working in the company. Each one of the members showed vulnerability and spoke openly and clearly. We used the SW (strengths and weakness) format, which allowed them to be more critical and flexible on their decision making. In about an hour the team reached the conclusion that their three main strengths are: flexibility, solid customer base and good position of the company in the industry. Their weaknesses: slow because of Dan's centralized decisions, working in silos, and don't know how to say no to customers.

Once they finished the exercise, we made good use of the moment of vulnerability among members, and we used the tool: distraction from the main responsibility.

Rony: Please write down in the following format your role and fundamental purpose, and then, all the activities that you perform at the company. Once you have a list of activities, you have to classify them in two parts: one with the activities that contribute to your main goal, and the other with the activities that distract you from your responsibilities. After identifying the activities that distract you, write the name of the person you think should be doing each one of them.

Dan: Could you give us an example of such activities? I think everything is important.

Rony: Yes, everything is important, but not everyone should be doing everything. For example, if Carlos from Sales, spends time with administration issues, he's not selling while he's distracted with that..

Alex: I get it. I think I can give another example. It's very common that people who work at Manufacture use the excuse of not finishing with the production committed because they are addressing the customer complaints. And while they're focused on the complaints, they can't manufacture on time.

Rony: That's a very good example.

Conclusions:

- To scale from self-employment to a company that doesn't depend on the CEO, you should build a team to whom you can delegate tasks and responsibilities and trust their smooth decision making.

- A key ingredient to building a team is to create a common "enemy," the simplest one that can be measured. A measurable and clear goal that should be reached with united efforts.

6 MEASURING PROGRESS.

> A pilot flying without a instrument panel faces many risks and lives stressed out.
>
> To have a dashboard not only shows the reality of the company, but also the contribution of each one of the members. Things are transparent. It shows which areas need more attention and support.

Rony: Before 1968, everyone around the world thought it was impossible to run 100 meters in less than 10 seconds. That is, until Jim Hines crossed that barrier for the first time, when he won the gold medal at the Mexico Olympic Games by running it in 9.95 seconds. He refuted every fake prophet who claimed that no man could travel more than 10 meters per second. He ran even faster and wasn't the only one. Now there are 126 more athletes who that have run the 100-meters in less than 10 amazing seconds. Today the record belongs to the Jamaican Usain Bolt, who ran it in 9.58 seconds.

Dan: And you're telling me this because…

Rony: In this story there are two elements that we should consider: 1. The limits we can impose on ourselves, and 2. The benefit of having a dashboard. Nobody believed someone could run the 100 meters in less than 10 seconds. Jim Hines did, and that's because he constantly measured his results and focused on improving a little each day, until he achieved it. Once he proved it was possible, people started believing, and almost immediately others achieved it too.

Dan: That's why world and Olympic records exist. The Olympics are fun to watch, also the dashboards and medal counts.

Rony: Do you have a dashboard that shows the development of your company and employees?

Dan: Yes, our bank account.

Rony: Unfortunately, that's not the best indicator because it doesn't matter if the bank account has or doesn't have money. That doesn't show the reality of the company, it just shows you've been flying blind and that every decision you've made has been based on your intuition and capacity for handling risks.

Dan: The amount of sales is the indicator I use the most, and which I use to brag about the company's success.

Rony: Nevertheless, a company that sells 1MD but has a profit of 20k is much less efficient than a company that bills 100k and has a profit of 10k. It's very common for companies that don't have a dashboard to experience much drama at the organization, because everyone reports differently, not concrete but emotional information. Numbers help the process become more rational, objective and quantitative.

Dan: You're right. At my company it's very complicated to have a detailed report or a fast update because we don't have the methodology of reporting or measuring results. When I ask Diana for her goals and emotional answers, she gives me a long list of written goals and not numbers. She doesn't give me the information that I need, and I have to walk around the office asking people what I need to know so I can complete the picture myself. I spend a lot of time being a researcher.

Rony: Definitely, having a **dashboard** will make your life easier. You're going to stop being a Detective and will have more objective information that will frame the reality of the company. The dashboard measures the pulse of the organization objectively and also gives you control. Once you register numbers for a certain period of time, you'll gain the ability to recognize patterns and tendencies that will help you predict the future.

Dan: Right now, I can't predict much. What I can tell you is that one night I'll wake up at 2 a.m with insomnia and a mental list of things to do at the company, without a clear idea of what should I fix first.

Rony: I'm sorry about your sleepless nights. It's a very common phenomenon among entrepreneurs and CEOs. I can't promise the dashboard is going to take the insomnia away, but it will give you a clearer picture of your company. You'll be able to focus on what really needs your attention.

Dan: Everything needs my attention right now.

Rony: How do you know where your attention should be if you don't have the right numbers?

Dan: I address what seems more urgent.

Rony: So, whoever knows how to manipulate your anxiety better, that's who you pay attention to? What about those members of the team that are too proud to ask for help, so they don't share with you if there's something urgent? Or those who are shy or don't trust you enough?

Dan: That's what happens with Victor. I have to ask him the department status many times, or unfortunately, I only pay attention when things become urgent or start getting out of control because he never tells me anything until the last minute. I feel I'm constantly putting out fires. Also with Alex, because he is shy and I feel he's scared of me, so I have to interrogate him like the CIA.

Rony: That's part of the problem. Without clear numbers we don't know where the **bottleneck** is.

Dan: What is the bottleneck, and which are the restrictions of the company?

Rony: It's a concept developed by Eliyahu Goldratt, that portrays how people should map the process of their companies, from the purchase of primary raw materials to the collection of it, going step by step and understanding the capacity of execution that each link at the company has. The bottleneck is the slowest phase, the phase that limits the complete process the most, and that determines the quantity of products or services we can provide.

For example, at a balloon factory, the machines can produce up to 1,000 pieces per hour, but if the printing area can only execute 800 pieces, this represents a bottleneck, because that's the total number of pieces that can be produced per day. An example of services could be an accounting firm, where each accountant has the capacity of meeting with five customers; if you have five accountants at the firm you have the installed capacity of meeting 25 customers; nevertheless, the person who works in administration can only carry the information of 20 customers, so our bottleneck here is the administration department. You should always search for the bottleneck to improve results of that area, process or person.

Dan: And once it improves, should I search for another one so we can be better and more efficient?

Rony: Right. Now tell me, what's your installed capacity?

Dan: 2 million packages per month.

Rony: That's the theoretical or real capacity? The theoretical is the one that appears in machine handbooks. The real one is the one you live with day by day, that can be affected by many elements like maintenance, employee training, workplace conditions and more.

Dan: Mmn, I don't know; I think that's the real capacity. Let me call Victor and ask him. He is the Production manager.

After 15 minutes of explanations, it still wasn't clear what the real capacity of the installation was. To make the situation worse, we called the director of Sales to find out how many packages the company sells per month.

Carlos: All that I can dispose of (answered arrogantly).

Rony: And how many are those?

Carlos: Mmn, as many as they provide.

Rony: Let me understand something You don't know how many packages you can sell?

Carlos: Yes, my goal is to sell 3 million packages per month... so 3 million.

I looked at Dan and asked him:

Rony: Do you see where the problem is? The Manufacturing department thinks they can produce 2 million as long as they reach the maximum capacity of machinery, and the Sales department says they can sell 3 million. Do you see the contradiction?

Dan: Now I know why these fellas don't get along or understand each other, as if they spoke different languages.

Rony: It's normal that CEOs don't like dashboards because it shows them the reality of their company and they would rather live thinking everything's fine. Some years ago, while walking in San Francisco, I found a sign that changed my way of thinking. It said: "The truth will set you free, but first it will piss you off". That's exactly what dashboards can provoke because they portray the reality, which will probably bother you. But trust me on this, it is better to have a reflection of reality that gives you control of your company, than living in a fantasy or with distress. If the captain of the Titanic had had a more complete dashboard, his decisions would have been very different.

The phrase: "You can't manage what you can't measure" is attributed to Peter Drucker. It's one of the most iconic phrases in the management world, used when we want to improve the efficiency of a company, team or person. As we mentioned before, progress makes you feel successful and measuring efforts gives you evidence of the progress or setbacks you've had. **If we're not reaching the desired results, KPIs will help us understand the reason and allow us to address it on time.** Otherwise, we'd be flying blind.

Can you imagine how complicated it would be for the pilot of an airplane to fly the aircraft without having altitude, wind direction or fuel indicators? It may be possible to fly a plane without a dashboard, but it's too risky and the pilot won't have the same level of trust or control over the aircraft. The same happens to the owners that operate their business without a dashboard that portrays the reality of their company. They act according to their instincts, in some cases, according to the complaints of customers, but most of them measure their companies according to their sales, which will help when making an evaluation, but won't give enough information. The sales number only shows vanity and pride,

while utilities reflect the effectiveness of the company. We should have a complete and integral dashboard that reflects reality as completely as possible to be able to make different decisions and evaluate their impact. These should be placed in a chart with the progress or setbacks.

Dan: Ok, I totally understand that. It's like a scale in the bathroom, which my wife calls "the liar". It doesn't matter if it lies or not, it reflects reality and shows whether the efforts to lose weight were effective.

Rony: I couldn't have explained it better.

By the way, do you know indicators are called KPIs?

Dan: Yes, but I don't know what it means.

Rony: It originally meant **key performance indicators (KPI)**, which are the numbers that demonstrate the development each person has in their roles at the company, but it can also be: *keep promises in place*: at the beginning of each quarter goals are established for everyone and they should accept those goals, which become their promise. It's also known as: *keep people informed*, because with indicators people can simply know the activities status.

Dan: I'm going to stay with: "keep promises in place", that's what I want for my company. I need to be surrounded by people that fulfil their commitments. I want to be certain that when there's a commitment, people will do even the impossible to fulfill it, and that I won't have to be chasing them to see if they complied with their activities. As I once told you, I'm a business leader, not a babysitter. I also have the problem of people giving me a lot of information, more than I need, which makes meetings longer and tedious.

Rony: For that, there's a formula you should implement. Each time someone presents their indicators, ask them the following questions, in the following order; that way, they'll get used to presenting standardized results that will help them think structured: The questions are:

❯ Color.

❯ Number.

❯ Why are you in that color?

〉 What's your plan to improve or maintain?

〉 What do you need from the team?

Dan: That's a great idea, because each person explains their results differently. Besides, I have a couple of members of the team that overtalk. They explain so many things that sometimes I can't even figure out if they're right or wrong.

Rony: Precisely. That's the idea, that you can understand the information easily and that everyone has a uniform way of thinking. If you noticed, these are systems or recipes that if someone replaces you, he only has to learn the methodology.

Let me tell you what happened with another one of my clients, Joe. He started his business of digital marketing and immediately started to have good results. He was selling and executing correctly. His customers were happy at the beginning, but suddenly, mistakes started to be made, customers started to complain or cancel their accounts, and money was falling short. That was when we decided he should implement a dashboard to understand what was happening to the company, stop living on the edge, and start solving the important things. The process of creating the dashboard was difficult, because first, he needed to define the right organizational structure based on the plans he had, and then hire the right people and measure their performance. We started in that order, because otherwise we might limit the potential of the company to the talent we have today. But after implementing a simple dashboard with only four KPIs per team member and another four for the people who reported to each member, a series of situations started happening at the company. For example, those people who don't like being measured or who are abusive were shown up by their numbers. So generally, these people leave the organization because they feel ashamed for not delivering results or because they feel under pressure to achieve a specific goal.

Dan: A few moments ago you mentioned **"color and number"**. What did you mean?

Rony: Dashboards are easier to read when you have concrete numbers and colors that help you visually identify things that require your attention. Traffic lights are the best example, and that's why we use those colors: red, yellow and green. What happens if the traffic lights are red?

Dan: You have to stop.

Rony: Yellow?

Dan: Caution. And green means carry on.

Rony: So, if we apply these colors to your KPIs on your dashboard, people should color their results (number). For example, if you have the goal of calling 100 prospects per week, you define it so that at least 90% of that goal would be green, between 80% and 89.99% would be yellow, and below 80% would be red. The person accountable for that indicator reports 81 calls were made.

Dan: The number should be 81 and the color yellow.

Rony: Correct. Going back to the example of the 100 meters at the Olympics. At the Beijing Olympics of 2008, Usain Bolt won gold for 9.69 seconds; Richard Thompson won silver for 9.89 seconds; Walter DX won bronze for 9.91 seconds; and Churandy Martina went home empty handed for almost nothing; he ran it in 9.93 seconds. If at the Olympics they identify results with colors, we can do the same at companies.

Dan: I understand, but it's going to look like a Christmas tree.

Rony: Probably, but you'll be able to fix the yellows and reds. Greens don't require much attention.

When implementing a dashboard and objectives for the first time, almost everything is either red or green. If everything's red it might be because the goals set were too high and aren't being fulfilled. If everything's green, probably the goals set were too low.

Dan: I believe that with time I'll realize if goals were high or low.

Rony: Exactly, but you'll need to have records that with time will become better at establishing, executing and measuring goals.

Dan: I wonder how our dashboard would look with traffic lights.

Rony: We'll find out soon enough. By the way, it's important that you clarify to your team that you want reality reflected on the dashboard, that if something's red they don't have to change it. People are afraid they might be fired because they turned out red, and their fear is well founded. But at the beginning of the process you can't take the risk of firing people because they turned out red on something that hasn't been measured before, something that we might be measuring wrong or for goals that might be set wrong too.

Dan: I know I have to create a safe environment where people feel confident showing the reality of the company.

Rony: And later, when people master this tool, if someone constantly turns out red he should definitely be working for the competition.

Dan: Ha ha, Bad employees can definitely go with the competition. By the way, can I copy the dashboard of another company? Why start from scratch?

Rony: Your dashboard has to be unique and special for your organization and needs. But I'll gladly show you the dashboard of another customer of mine, to inspire you.

Dan: Ok, where do I start?

Rony: I need you to join your team for this exercise.

Dan: I would like you to lead the exercise.

Rony: I know you can do it. Whatever result you get is better than what you have today. It will be a victory you won together with your team. Meet your team for about two hours at a place where you won't be interrupted, where you can write on flip charts or screen your Excel on a big screen so that everyone can see what's happening. The steps are:

Step 1: Create a **matrix** with the following columns. Who, Role, KPI, Goal, dates.

				January				February				March				
Who	Role	Kpi	Goal	5	12	19	26	2	9	16	23	2	9	16	23	30

Step 2: Context. Explain the context to your team with the following story: we are a team that works remotely and by the nature of our operation, there's not much to talk about We only have to show the numbers that give us the real pulse of the organization. We only communicate with numbers.

Step 3: Success indicators according to fundamental purpose. According to the structural organization that you have already, each one of the positions that has figured out what their success indicator is should be the first KPI per person, on the KPI column.

Step 4: Complementary indicators. Every member of the team should have complementary indicators or previous steps to reach their success indicators. Write them in the KPI column.

Step 5: Responsible and in charge. When you have your success and complementary indicators, you should put the name of the person responsible for them and his position in the respective columns. Write only one name on each.

Step 6: Establish the objective to reach that quarter.

Step 7: Start applying the dashboard from that week on.

Step 8: Settle traffic lights rule, red, yellow, green and super green colors. These will reflect your goals according to the results.

Dan: The steps are clear for me. The next time we meet I'll show you what we achieved. If I get stuck with something I'll call you.

Rony: In the meantime, tell me which number you can be obsessed with from the beginning of the process, that will give a sense of progress and also guide the efforts to achieve a specific goal. It could be sales, pieces, or any other number that reflects success at the organization.

Dan: Right now, the number that I feel is worse with the situation we have now at the organization is cash flow. I want to increase that number to live peacefully.

Rony: For the first draft of your dashboard you'll have 25 to 30 KPIs. If you feel it's not complete, add the KPI's you think are convenient. Try maintaining the dashboard with a maximum of 30 KPIs for a team of six members. Later on, you'll want to have a smaller dashboard, with 6 or 7 key indicators that will show the status and reality of the company, and that will be meaningful when you make a decision.

Dan: Right now I'll be happy if we have a dashboard that reflects individual development and the status of the organization, even with 30 indicators.

Rony: With the dashboard each member will have an objective way to demonstrate their progress at the organization, and with that information, you'll be able to give them feedback and coaching so they can improve their results.

Dan: For sure, it will be more transparent and objective. Now I'm going to know for sure who delivers good results and who doesn't.

Rony: Besides, each person will focus on doing what they have to do.

Dan: That's what I want. It's very annoying when someone from my team is doing everything but nothing effectively. Alex is always busy, but I don't know how effective he is; my intuition tells me he's not.

Rony: You'll be tempted to remove or add indicators in the first quarter. Please don't remove any indicator because you need to have a record to start noticing tendencies and predicting performance.

Dan: Duly noted. I'll commit with the team to keep the dashboard intact for 3 months. At the end of that quarter we'll decide if we need to remove or add any indicator.

A friend of mine that invests in the market told me that people invest in companies listed on the Exchange that establish their goals and fulfill them each quarter. That shows a committed team that works together and accomplishes what they promise.

Rony: I'm going to share with you some **benefits** that can be obtained from having a dashboard.

❿ Numbers remove subjective and vague communication.

❿ An environment of accountability is created.

❿ Commitment and clarity.

❿ Feeling of healthy competition.

❿ Control and visibility.

❿ Teamwork.

❿ Problems are solved faster and more effectively.

❿ You can identify the areas that require immediate assistance.

Rony: When implementing KPIs the team feels frustrated because they don't know how to measure their results, but this happens with any new skill. At the beginning you might feel frustrated for not knowing how to master it as you do with others. For example, if you are learning to play the guitar, even if you know how to play the piano, at the beginning you feel a high level of frustration because you aren't mastering playing the guitar. Frustration is good evidence when learning something new. We shouldn't mistake frustration with things not working out. As Tony Robbins says: "Welcome, frustration."

To reduce drama at the organization, you have to implement a dashboard that shows the reality of the company. You may not like what you see at the beginning, but it's the only way to evaluate your progress. Like the scale in the bathroom at your house, you don't like what you see, but you should be thankful that you have a tool that provides useful information so you can make accurate decisions and stop living in a fantasy.

Conclusions:

❯ When you're at the point where you can measure performance and have clarity of your reality and operation, you can demand results from your team and put into practice the philosophy of "accountability".

 THE ART OF BEING PROTAGONIST.

> ❯ Adam and Eve were punished and banished from Paradise not for breaking a rule, but for not being accountable for their actions. They blamed each other instead of accepting their responsibility, and as a punishment, they were banished so they could learn the lesson of being accountable for their actions.
>
> ❯ The magic ingredient that can transform any culture is "taking responsibility" or "being accountable." Being surrounded by people who are responsible for their actions and their results makes it possible to work towards a common objective without people setting back progress.

A couple of weeks after we last met, Dan proudly presented his dashboard to me.

Dan: I want to show you my dashboard. It has been a difficult task. We had a hard time starting to measure; besides, we had to add indicators we hadn't before, that I thought were missing.

Rony: With time you'll probably add more and then we'll clean it up, because you'll need a simple dashboard, like the dashboard of your car. Only a couple of numbers can give you the complete picture.

Dan was happy with the progress his company was making thanks to the methodology. He had a clearer language, clearer roles, and indicators; nevertheless, he was very frustrated because some members of his team were justifying their low performance or blaming other people for it.

Dan: What will be the surprise now that we're meeting at a fast food place?

Rony: Do you see those stuffed trash cans?

Dan: Yes, it seems people here don't care much for cleaning.

Rony: I've come here many times not for the incredible culinary arts, but for a very interesting phenomenon. There are four people in charge of cleaning, and their names are: Everyone, Someone, Anyone and Nobody. There's an important job to do, cleaning the trash cans. *Everyone* was sure *Someone* would do it. *Anyone* could have done it, but *Nobody* did. *Someone* got angry about it because it was *Everyone's* job. *Everyone* thought *Anyone* could do it, but *Nobody* realized that *Anyone* wouldn't do it. This story ended with *Everyone* blaming *Someone* because *Nobody* did what *Anyone* could do.

Dan: I think I understand the story, but it's a bit confusing.

Rony: No problem, let's change the name of Everyone for Alex, Someone for Diana,

Anyone for Carlos and Nobody for Victor. There's an important job to do, cleaning the trash cans. *Alex* was sure *Diana* would do it. *Carlos* could have done it, but *Victor* didn't do it. *Diana* got angry about it because it was *Alex's* job. *Alex* thought *Carlos* could do it, but *Victor* realized that *Carlos* wouldn't do it. This story ended with *Alex* blaming *Diana* because *Victor* didn't do what *Carlos* could do. As you can see, in the end nothing was achieved, because everyone assumed someone else would do it.

Dan: This story describes correctly some moments I have experienced at the company. Many tasks end up in no man's land and they blame each other, forgetting that in the end, Plastypack will suffer the consequences.

Rony: It's very difficult to generate a nice and permanent progress in an environment where there's no culture of **accountability**.

Dan: It's impossible to make progress with people not taking responsibility for their actions, people keep telling me any number of stories to explain why they didn't fulfill their tasks. I don't care why they

couldn't fulfill them, I'm only interested in having things done. People give their word lightly at this company: they say they're going to hand in a report on the 20th and they don't. They say they're going to respect the program of customer deliveries and they don't. It's impossible to work like that.

Rony: Can you give me an example?

Dan: Victor is either lying or modifying his KPIs only to look good, but he's not letting me see the reality of the company, because the company isn't reaching its goals. He puts things on green that should be red or yellow, but he justifies it by saying he tried his best and puts things on green.

Rony: Give me more information.

Dan: For example, he has the goal of fulfilling 95% of the production plan; his result was 88% which is red for us, but he puts it on green because he says the manufacturing plan changed according to the needs of the commercial area, so for him, it is green.

Rony: Yes, Victor lies about his KPIs to look good. This happens because he puts his personal interests before the interests of the company. He's not taking responsibility or being accountable for his actions. This is something you shouldn't allow on the team. Information has to be transparent, reflecting reality, so you can make the right corrections. The purpose is to fix mistakes, not to look good.

In Nestlé, we had goals linked to bonus: 40% to individual development, 30% to division development and 30% to the results of the organization. How would you explain that the bonus was given to every employee of every division and the organization wasn't fulfilling its results? In some cases goals weren't linked correctly, in others, bosses qualified bad results as good; in other cases people lied, etc. To conclude, KPIs indicate the reality of the company. Once you have clarity with your results you can jump to the step of rewarding, developing or punishing employees according to their development.

Dan: I have to be tougher with the team. Results should reflect reality, not their vanity or excuses.

Rony: The word **accountability** sometimes tends to be mixed with responsibility, but these two concepts are different. This generates confusion in many companies. The best way to understand the difference is with this example: a 16-year-old boy who has his driver's license asks his father if he can take the car, and his father agrees. The boy had a car accident. Who's responsible for this accident?

Dan: The boy. No wait, I think both.

Rony: See? It's confusing and not easy to distinguish. If instead of asking who's responsible I ask: who has to be accountable for the accident?

Dan: That question is simpler. The father has to be accountable before the authorities.

Rony: Right. But the boy is responsible for the accident.

Dan: The boy is accountable at home with his father.

Rony: Exactly. The same happens at companies. If the department of Carlos doesn't meet the expected results because of Patrick, who reports to him, Carlos is accountable for the results before you and the leadership team, even if Patrick was responsible for it. Everything depends on the perspective of who to be accountable to.

Dan: It's very difficult to be surrounded by people who don't take responsibility or are accountable for their actions! People who keep blaming others for their own mistakes. I remember a friend of mine that was always on a diet, and most of the time he blamed the nutritionist for his situation, but nobody forced him to eat anything.

Rony: Yes, it is simpler to blame others than to be accountable. Putting it simply, to be accountable is to keep your promises. Human beings are specialized in the art of lying to ourselves, procrastinating and "excusitis," and that's why it's not easy to change our habits or our lives. Nevertheless, there are ways of changing. Alcoholics Anonymous has developed a simple and effective methodology that starts with…

Dan: Recognizing the fact of being alcoholic.

Rony: Exactly. The program simply consists of recognizing it and not drinking that day.

Dan: One day at a time, as they say.

Rony: That's right, keep your promise day by day.

Dan: You know what drives me crazy? People who don't keep their promises. When I remember what they committed to, it is either too late or it has become an urgent matter.

Rony: The worst thing is that when someone enters your office, you make an agreement and it's your responsibility to follow it up, and you never do. You already have many things to do and personal concerns to follow up, as well as remembering every commitment to which your employees committed.

Dan: You're describing exactly how I feel. Many people pass through my office every day and all of them make commitments or agree to do many things, and I can't follow up on everything. I'm not their babysitter, I expect them to be professional and that if they give their word on something they keep it.

Rony: Here's a tool that will help you a lot with this problem, it's called an **action plan**, which consists of three different columns: who, what and when. Each time someone makes a commitment it has to be written here in his hand so there are no excuses. Do you remember a while ago I presented the format where you write what, who and when?

Dan: Of course, I didn't remember it was called an **action plan** but we've used it already. It sounds too good to be true. Will something that simple help me solve something that complex?

Rony: I understand your concern, but sometimes the simpler the better. Have you ever heard about the **KISS methodology**?

Dan: The rock band that paints their faces and uses large boots? I'm dying to go to one of their concerts before some member dies.

Ha ha ha, we both laughed

Rony: No, not the band KISS, the methodology; which means **keep it simple stupid**.

Dan: Yes, I have to accept that sometimes I make my life harder than it should be. Your action plan tool sounds good, but the list will be long.

Rony: Don't worry. At the beginning it will be long, but later on people will make fewer commitments. It's very important that they write them down and you follow them up when they expire. If you don't follow them up and probably give them a consequence when they expire, this won't work.

Dan: So now I have to become an executioner? Punishing everyone?

Rony: Ha ha ha, no. By consequence I mean implementing something you think is convenient, not an actual punishment. Consequences can be either positive or negative. Examples of negative consequences: doing a one push-up for every day of delay in front of the team, or buying coffee for the entire team. Examples of positive consequences: acknowledge an employee who fulfilled commitments. That way, people's behavior will change and they will change too, there's a formula for it.

Dan: I don't believe you Rony! I've been married for 15 years and my wife hasn't changed a bit.

Rony: Of course she has changed! Maybe not the way you wanted, but surely she has. The technique I'm going to share with you is very simple, but you have to be constant. But first I'm going to give you an example. Can a Mexican citizen change in 15 minutes?

Dan: No.

Rony: Of course he can. He only has to cross the border to the USA and his behavior will change immediately. Suddenly, we become more civilized, we stop the car at the STOP signs while driving, we're more friendly and don't throw anything from the window to the ground. Why? How can you explain this phenomenon?

Dan: Because in the USA people are stricter about law and order.

Rony: Exactly. You're on the right path. The US has rules (laws), with consequences and when they're broken they are executed, and that's why these rules are respected.

Dan: Right, that's why Mexico is a chaos, they don't have any of those three.

Rony: That's incorrect, Mexico has rules (laws) and consequences. The problem consists of the third factor, executing the consequence.

Without this one, the system fails. Here's what you should do: you should talk to your team about the action plan and the consequences in case of not meeting their commitments and commit to apply the consequence to the person who breaks any rule.

Dan: It's like threatening a kid and not abiding by the threat. One of my kids has me totally figured out. He knows my threats are never carried out, so he always does whatever he wants.

Rony: That's why we have to be careful with what we say. If you want people to keep their promises you have to be the example. If you make a threat about something you have to abide by it, especially if it's to yourself, because you have to set an example. It's time to be more demanding with your team.

Dan: I know, it's one of my weaknesses. I make so many exceptions that now it has become a rule.

Rony: Now's the time for you to have rules and also exceptions.

Dan: I don't get it, have rules and also exceptions?

Rony: From now on, you'll hear me repeat this philosophy a lot because until now, your super entrepreneur flexibility has let you make exceptions with everything: you adapt to all your customers, suppliers, and employees. But from now on, I want you to have rules, and these will have their exceptions. For example, if the rule is that the maximum amount of time of the available credit line for customers is 45 days, maybe you'll need to make an exception with an important customer and extend it to 60 days, but for the rest of the customers, that can't be an option. It's better to have an exception than having different credit lines for each customer, this drives the administration team crazy, and above all, sacrifices your cash flow.

Dan: My wife says something similar about our kid's education. It's better to always have boundaries and from now on be a little flexible. At our home, our kids can't drink sodas, but when they go to their grandma's house every Friday they can have one soda. Our kids know the rule, but sometimes they want to drink another soda during the week, and once in a while we let them. Before they drank soda often and

that was the rule instead of the exception. It makes sense that everyone has to adapt to me or the company and not the other way around.

Rony: I'm sure you're exhausted from the different agreements and concessions you have with your employees.

Dan: I can't even tell you how much. Employees know I have a good heart, so they come to me and ask for permissions and raises because they know it is hard for me to say no.

Rony: I'm not telling you to always say no, but you have to be clear about permissions, salaries and company rules. If someone needs an exception, you'll think about it; on the contrary, it is standardized.

By the way, let me be clear about the word "consequence." It's a word that has acquired a negative connotation with time, as well as the word "conflict." A consequence is the result of something. Do you remember when at school they taught you the third Law of Newton?

Dan: **For every action, there is an equal or opposite reaction.** Ha ha ha, I had no idea I still had that information on my personal software.

Rony: Exactly, a consequence is a reaction that can be either positive or negative. We have assumed with time that a consequence and/or reaction is negative. If you plant a seed, the consequence is that it will grow and a plant will blossom. If you punch a stranger on the street, surely...

Dan: I'll have serious issues when my wife finds out I was arrested by the police.

Ha ha ha, we both laughed.

Rony: Let's take accountability to the next level. Now that we have a dashboard with traffic light colors, what would be the maximum consequence of the person who constantly appears in red?

Dan: Get fired.

Rony: Which would be the maximum consequence of the person who constantly appears in yellow?

Dan: Mmn, I don't know.

Rony: In that case you have to support that person to make a change. Maybe he has a problem at home or needs training or something else.

When someone's yellow we have to identify what's happening and help him/her get past yellow. In case he doesn't make it, eventually he will turn red, and if that's the case, you had better give them the opportunity to have a brilliant future at another company. And what would be the maximum consequence of a person that constantly appears in green?

Dan: A raise or a bonus (he said enthusiastically).

Rony: No, you can acknowledge or congratulate that person, but a raise or bonus? Are you not paying them enough to always be green? Now you can understand why you have a disaster with the payroll at your company, because each time someone does what they should do and asks for a raise, you touch your heart and give them that raise. That's something we should talk about another day. I'm pro rewards, prizes, bonuses and raises, but these will be given as long as people arrive at the "extra mile" or become super green. Something has to prove that this person has added more value, and you're willing to reward the extra added value.

Dan: I get the idea. I hope this dashboard really provides important information.

Rony: Let's talk about the autonomy of decisions. Do you remember a few months ago we mentioned autonomy goes hand in hand with responsibilities?

Dan: My team has the autonomy to make decisions.

Rony: That's perfect! That means every member contributes something they're good at to the company. Employees have to have the autonomy of decision making in their areas of responsibility, so the company's culture of accountability persists. For example, when you ask someone to make a report, that would be the **what**. Do you also tell them **how** to do it?

Dan: Yes, on some occasions I tell them **how** to do it.

Rony: Perhaps **how** to do it is not why you hire someone? If you take your car to the agency for maintenance (**what**), do you tell them **how** to do it?

Dan: Of course not, they're specialized on **how** to do it. I get it. My employees have to be specialized in how they do things and I have to set the goals, or in this case, the **what**, and they should establish the **how.** And what happens when they don't know **how** to do it or I simply don't like the way they do it?

Rony: You can always teach them how. No one said you "let them loose", you only have to minimize telling them **how** they should do things. You can be very surprised about how the organization will progress on its decision making when people know their decisions are independent and that they have to be accountable based on their results.

Dan: Excuses will be over at the company.

Conclusions:

❶ When their word matters to employees, culture transforms and the company is guided towards good results. Everything becomes more predictable because people do what they say they'd do.

❶ Considering that people will comply with what they promise, you have to incorporate an element that aligns your team and is goal oriented: work meetings.

 8 EXECUTIVE MEETINGS.

> "The only thing more harmful than facing an awkward issue is pretending it doesn't exist." Patrick Lencioni.

We gathered early in the morning at one of Best Buy stores, right at the opening hour.

Dan: So this time you brought me to buy electronic equipment for the office? I know that my printers aren't new and my office needs an air conditioner. I didn't know your coaching services were also for technological support.

We both laughed.

Rony: Good! You found another purpose to this visit. Actually, we came to observe the Best Buy staff daily meeting.

Employees dressed in khaki pants and blue polo shirts gathered around the cash register and stood there. The staff radiated energy and happiness. A couple of members started sharing personal good news, to which everyone applauded. Suddenly, an employee approached us.

Alan: Good morning, my name is Alan, can I help you with something?

Rony: Thanks, we're waiting for Frank.

Alan: Perfect, I'll let him know you're waiting, and when our meeting finishes he'll come right away. If you need anything else, please let me know.

The employee smiled at us and went back to the meeting. Then, we were able to hear how each department reported its numbers, discussed some critical business issues and at the end, sang a song together. The meeting lasted 13 minutes and 20 seconds. When it finished, Frank, the store manager, approached us.

Frank: It's so good to see you today Rony! Long time no see; seems life has treated you well! You gained some pounds and grey hairs.

Rony: Yes, life has been good to me. I've been a bit careless with my eating habits, but now I'm on a good diet and exercise plan to get back in shape. You look happy Frank. I hope things are good at work and also at home.

Frank: To be honest, I can't complain. Things are better than ever. Aren't you going to introduce me to your friend?

Rony: Of course! Dan's the CEO of a company that I'm working with right now. I'm coaching him to grow and scale up his company.

Dan: It's very nice meeting you Frank.

Frank: You are in good hands. Rony coached and helped me personally in a process of leadership at the company where I was working at the time. I'm sure you came with a particular purpose.

Rony: Yes, we're working on **the Meeting rhythm.**

Dan: I don't even know why we are addressing this topic. Meetings are a waste of time, inefficient and excessive. I don't see the point of having more meetings than we have today.

Frank: I used to think just like you. I was overwhelmed with the quantity of meetings we had, where people talked about everything and never reached any conclusion. It was a waste of time and money; and even worse, people were distracted from their day-to-day activities and responsibilities.

Dan: Precisely. While people are at the meeting they're not doing what they have to. Besides, the same situations are repeated in each meeting without making any progress. People talk but I don't see any result.

Frank: Maybe the problem isn't that you have many meetings which are distracting and make the organization unproductive. The problem is that your meetings probably aren't effective.

Dan: How do you know my meetings aren't effective?

Frank: Because if they were, you would have fewer meetings, decisions would be made, progress would be evident, and employees would expect to attend the meetings enthusiastically.

Dan: You're right.

Frank: In some way, we're all to blame because we never learned how to address meetings correctly. I'm sure Rony told you already that you should use meetings effectively, and he's right. Meetings are inevitable for companies, even necessary, but they have to be executed correctly to be effective. As you can see, a few minutes ago we had our daily meeting where we sought to align every member with the most practical and important information we have today, like in football. Between plays, the team has very brief meetings where they decide and agree on the next play.

Dan: I'm a big fan of the NFL. It's amazing how much they share and the decisions they make in just a few seconds.

Frank: You can do the same at your company, but maybe not in 15 seconds. We held daily meetings of 15 minutes a day. We're not the only ones who do this; if you go to Wal-Mart, you will see they do it too; they have a meeting before each shift where they share their daily goals. Restaurants also do it; before starting their daily operations waiters meet for 15 minutes to be aware of critical information like the products that they won't have that day or if they only have a few, so they will be careful when selling them. I really care about measuring the pulse of my team, knowing what they're going through personally, how they are progressing with their results, and that we are always united as a single team.

Dan: But the time you use for your meeting is time you're not dedicating to your customers, and that can be very expensive.

Frank: It's even more expensive that employees make mistakes or are not aligned. Besides, during our meeting, there are always assigned employees to be watching in case any customer arrives, like Alan who approached you today. It's an ability that can be developed to achieve better results at a company, to make people responsible for their commitments, measure progress, and correct employee behavior.

Rony: Not every meeting is the same Each has different objectives and agendas.

Frank: It can be overwhelming at the beginning, but once you understand the right structure and how to execute them, it becomes simple. When meetings are always effective, you realize you can't live without them; besides, meetings that today seem crucial will become unnecessary.

Dan: And how can I achieve that?

Frank: Rony will show you a way for sure, he has more experience than me. Besides, I have to go to my weekly meeting with the store managers. We do it virtually because it's also very important to be on the same page on a company level and see how we can help each other between stores. Dan, it was very nice meeting you.

Dan: Thank you for your time.

We shook hands and he said goodbye with a big smile.

Dan: It seems he's a great guy and I'm excited knowing people think meetings are useful. I'm still a little skeptical on how to make them effective.

Rony: Nowadays, you have many meetings at your company and most of them happen spontaneously, which makes them reactive instead of proactive.

Dan: Each time we have meetings I see how people are distracted and bored. I prefer to go to the floor where I can speed things up and solve them, even if it depends on me.

Rony: You hit the nail on the head., That's your biggest problem. Your meetings aren't attractive, fun or productive, and that's why you and your team avoid them at any cost.

Dan: Can meetings be fun and productive?

Rony: Of course. Moreover, the higher the position on the structure of the organization, the more important your results on meetings are. They're part of your operational activities. People who are more functional, like laborers in the manufacturing plant, should have fewer meetings, like the sellers at Best Buy; but as you go up in the hierarchy, you should have more meetings with different objectives and agendas. Most importantly, make sure the company is making progress.

Dan: As football players would say: "move the ball forward".

Rony: According to an article written by Linda LeBlanc and Melissa R. Nosik, specialized in behavior analysis, people spend more than 50% of their time at work meetings. This information was also confirmed by Patrick Lencioni, a great business consultant who revealed that company executives spend a lot of time at work meetings which, unfortunately, don't have the right elements to be effective or productive. A company that has a right and effective rhythm of meetings provokes accountability and responsibility between team members, because no one wants to be exposed for not delivering results.

Dan: What are the elements? If there's a solution, I want to know it.

Rony: You have to consider the following 6 steps:

1. **Establishing an agenda.** Each meeting has a particular purpose. Attendees have to know the reason, duration, location and who will be at the meeting. That way, they can prepare and anticipate, to avoid talking about things that aren't aligned to the meeting.

2. **Meeting attendees.** You have to be selective with the attendees; if you have more people than you should, it can be confusing and distracting. Only the people you need should be there.

3. **Meeting site.** You should have a site reserved for the meeting, either physical or virtual. It can be either by phone or digital; like Zoom, Goto Meeting, Google Meet or other platforms.

4. **Meeting leader or facilitator.** There should always be a leader at the meeting. It makes it simpler; someone who's watching the agenda and time.

5. **Action plan.** The document we have mentioned before, where the commitments of the attendees are written. At the end of each meeting commitments that ensure the progress of the organization have to be made.

6. **Dashboard.** Have access to the numbers that help making decisions.

Dan: Definitely, our meetings don't meet these points. Each meeting has more people attending than it should have, and these people distract the others or are only wasting time. We talk endlessly without reaching any result, we can spend a lot of time without making any decision. You said each meeting has an agenda.

Rony: Yes, the Verne Harnish methodology of "Scale up" presents five types of meetings that can give the company the right rhythm to accelerate decision making.

Type of meeting	Time required	Purpose	Agenda	Keys to success
Daily	15 minutes	Synchronization. Understanding organizational needs to operate effectively.	1. Good news. 2. kpis and/or metrics. 3. What are you stuck with? 4. Action plan. 5. Closure.	1. Standing assistants. 2. Access to dashboard. 3. Action plan. 4. Don't cancel the meeting if some members can't attend 5. Fix place and time.
Weekly	60 to 90 minutes	Tactical. Review weekly progress, metrics, and solving tactical situations.	1. Good news. 2. kpis and/or metrics. 3. Customers' and employees' feedback. 4. Quarter priority. 5. Action plan. 6. Closure.	1. Access to dashboard. 2. Action plan. 3. Place and time previously set. 4. Promote healthy conflict. 5. Postpone strategic topics.
Monthly	2 to 4 hours	Strategy and Development. Discuss, analyze, brainstorm and decide critical issues that affect success on a long term.	1. Good news. 2. kpis and/or metrics. 3. Action plan. 4. Progress of quarter goals. 5. Priority 1. 6. Priority 2. 7. Action plan. 8. Learning or training. 9. Closure.	1. Access to dashboard. 2. Action plan. 3. Place and time previously set. 4. Promote healthy conflict. 5. Prepared results by department.
Quarterly	8 to 16 hours	Strategy and Development. Review strategy, industry tendencies, competitive overview, key staff, team development.	1. Good news. 2. Quarter results. 3. Analysis of lessons and victories of Q. 4. Training. 5. Goal definition of next Q. 6. Action plan. 7. Closure.	1. Access to dashboard. 2. Action plan. 3. Place and time previously set. 4. Promote healthy conflict. 5. Prepared results by department and of the company. 6. Held the meeting out of the office.
Annual	8 to 16 hours	Strategy and Development. Review strategy, industry tendencies, competitive overview, key staff, team development.	1. Good news. 2. Year results. 3. Analysis of lessons and victories of the year. 4. Training. 5. Goal definition for next year. 6. Goal definition for next quarter. 7. Action plan. 8. Closure.	1. Access to dashboard. 2. Action plan. 3. Place and time previously set. 4. Promote healthy conflict. 5. Preparation of results per department and of the company. 6. Held the meeting out of the office.

Rony: The effective combination of dashboards and meetings might be one of the most important elements to let you have the organization under control. At the beginning you don't have to implement these five types of meetings. Most of my clients start on their own with a weekly or daily meeting. When you're able to control one of these two meetings, you'll start to see magical results. As for me, I'll facilitate some of the monthly meetings, so you can see how it's done, and while we work together I'll also facilitate all your quarterly and annual meetings.

Dan: Right now, I commit to implementing weekly meetings. I think that's not going to be overwhelming.

Rony: Perfect. Little changes will make the difference.

Dan: I hope this rhythm helps me reduce the number of meetings I have nowadays.

Rony: It definitely will. When people know there's a particular moment when their worries will be listened to, they'll wait for the meeting to talk about what they need, and only in exceptional cases you'll have complementary meetings to solve specific issues.

Conclusions:

- Meetings are an effective tool when used correctly. They let you maintain the pulse of the organization, team synchronization and above all, a culture of accountability, because at every meeting commitments have to be made and then reviewed at the next meeting. This is an effective way of keeping track of the progress of the company and of its collaborators.

- Now that you are aware of the fundamental basis that gives you vision, clarity and commitment towards the company, you'll be ready to let go of customers, suppliers, products and employees that no longer contribute to the organization.

9 CORE BUSINESS: WHAT IS THE MAIN REASON OF THE BUSINESS AND THE ADDED VALUE TO ITS CLIENTS?

> ❯ "I fear not the man who has practiced 10,000 kicks once, but I fear the man who has practiced one kick 10,000 times". Bruce Lee.
>
> ❯ The CEO has to recognize the business's main reason and the value he adds to his clients to be more efficient and effective. He has to make sure that every activity, effort, resource and objective is oriented to satisfying the primary need of his clients.

Rony: We've already traveled part of this journey of growth and organizational development. The concept **"core business"** is going to help you discover what's your main business. Have you ever heard the expression "Mind your own business"?

Dan: Yes, of course.

Rony: The **core business** of an organization is an idealized construct intended to express the organization's "main" or "essential" activity.

Core business process means that a business's success depends not only on how well each department performs its work, but also on how well the company manages to coordinate departmental activities to conduct the core business process

Dan: The theory makes sense, but the practice will be difficult.

Rony: It's not difficult if you understand your core business and stick to it. For example, on May 30th 2020, the space rocket Falcon 9 was launched, with the spacecraft Crew Dragon, that left from the NASA installations in Florida.

Dan: Yes I know. My kids were very excited to see the launch and hear the stories of the American astronauts. They're already dreaming of being astronauts. It reminded me of the stories my parents told me about the first man who walked on the moon.

Rony: Well, there's a very important lesson to learn about the story of this recent launch. This was the first time NASA sent astronauts from American soil after decades of using Russian services. NASA realized that they're not specialized in designing and manufacturing spacecraft, so they hired the services of Boeing and SpaceX, both specialized in creating motors and spacecrafts. These two companies were competing to create the spacecraft that was going to be used for the next trip to space. It's the first time that private companies are involved in the process of sending astronauts to outer space. If this mission succeeds, a new era of commercial trips to space will begin.

Dan: I assumed that this project was completely NASA. I never imagined they outsourced companies to do something as important as manufacturing a spacecraft.

Rony: Well, we're living a moment of change. Everyone is opening their eyes to understand what they're really good at. NASA has the right knowledge and team to make calculations and operate missions, but they're not very effective with transportation.

Dan: Interesting. Maybe that's the answer to why the Boeing airline disappeared. Before, they operated commercial flights and then the airline disappeared; nevertheless, many aircraft that we use nowadays are still produced by Boeing. I'm sure they applied the core business concept.

Rony: Gary Hamel and C. K. Prahalad, in their book *Competing for the Future*, presented diversified corporations as a gigantic tree: the main products are the trunk, the main limbs of business units are the branches, and the finished products are the leaves. Core business is the root system that gives nourishment and stability; it's what the organization essentially knows about manufacturing, coordination and technology.

Dan: It's knowing what I do better than others. I remember I read a similar case of success. It was about Honda. They are very good at manufacturing motors, so they do it for cars, lawn mowers and electric plants.

Rony: Exactly. Honda is a great example of this. its core business is manufacturing motors and they have pushed their potential to the limit, to the point where trying to copy what they do is very hard. This gives them a benefit they can use over and over again, giving them competitive advantages ahead of other brands.

Dan: Yes, they capitalized their knowledge, which came from the experience they had from the evolution of manufacturing motors since motorcycles.

Rony: Knowing your core business prevents mistakes that can put the company at risk, like outsourcing operations. Every company can, and I would dare to say, should outsource the activities of the company that are not essential or part of their core, because if you are specialized in manufacturing packages, you should outsource the services of logistics and transportation, which aren't as important as production. Because as much as you try you won't become excellent at something that is not part of your core business, which in this case is packaging production.

Dan: Talking about cars, Chrysler thought motors were a luxury for a while, so they outsourced the manufacturing of their motors to Mitsubishi and Hyundai. This made them lose their competitive advantage.

Rony: I can see you're a fan of cars.

Dan: Yes I am. There's so much passion involved in a car race, an aligned and well shaped team, machinery ready, a sense of competition, performance indicators everywhere; it's like watching the development of a company and its results very fast, without having to wait an entire quarter to see the results.

Rony: Your analogy is very interesting. Seeing it that way, if a career that lasts only a couple of hours it can indicate many things

in perspective. Your business can indicate these things in months. In my case, I love board games and I incorporated some in the coaching process for teams. Only in a few minutes a bunch of elements and phenomena that happen at the company can be simulated. Like when we did the workshop of "We're all in the same boat", its purpose is to show the importance of collaboration and the elements to achieve it.

Dan: Yes, that was a fun session. About that...I have to be honest, at the beginning when I saw you coming with a board game and you started setting the pieces, I thought you were crazy. But once I saw the interaction of the team, the decision making, the conflicts that are only on the surface merging in a controlled and fun situation, it was amazing. It gave me a lot of information about the personality and dynamics of my team. It removed friction and trained them.

Rony: I'm glad you liked it. I really enjoy board games. I think that **non-formal education,** like board games, can have many benefits and teach many things.

Dan: I'm looking forward to the workshop where we're learning strategy and negotiation. We're also going to use a board game, right?

Rony: Yes, it is. The workshop's name is: "Building my way." But going back to the core business, I have the impression that the concept is clear. So, what is the core business of your company?

Dan: Manufacturing and selling packages.

Rony: Sorry to interrupt you Dan, but when I was walking through your warehouse I saw some cleaning products; the forklift guys told me you sell those too.

Dan: That's true, we also sell cleaning products.

Rony: Any other product or service apart from the packages I should know about?

Dan: Yes, we develop web pages. Our marketing department has some free time, so I decided to use that time to sell web pages.

Rony: Dan, do you realize the diversification you have and how little your products support one another? You remind me of a cartoon I saw a while ago in the newspaper: a man opened his raincoat and inside

it you could find all kinds of services, like plumbing, insurance sales, gardening, etc. When you have so much variety, you're not recognized as an expert on anything.

Dan: Well, I guess you're right, but we had to survive somehow. I've had to incorporate other products to have more money to survive each month. Also, one of my most important customers asked us to help him find cleaning material and I couldn't say no. Imagine if I said no and he canceled our contract. I was cutting corners.

Rony: This is not unusual at all. The pressure of not having sufficient cash flow to continue daily operations often leads to searching for different sources of income, and it's also difficult to say NO, especially to your biggest client. Did providing these services make your operation complicated?

Dan: You have no idea how much! Now it's more difficult to operate. There are many SKUs, more raw material, more suppliers, etc.

Rony: Which one of those products is the most profitable?

Dan: Mmn, I don't know, but I suppose the packages because I manufacture them.

Rony: Let's suppose you're removing all the other products that aren't packages. Will that make you more efficient? Would your sales team perform better?

Dan: Yes, definitely.

Rony: Ok, and how many types of packages do you have?

Dan: Lots! Each client has a different one.

Rony: Ok, now's the time for us to think about your interests, to find a way for you to be more efficient and also satisfy your customer needs. That's why we have to *simplify and standardize* the operation as much as we can. That will prevent mistakes, fuzzy efforts and a bad image that you may have in the market for being Jack-of-all-trades. Further on, we'll get deeper into simplifying and standardizing. I should tell you that you'll get rid of products, customers, suppliers and even employees. It sounds worse than it is, but we'll do it step by step. First, we should return to your core business, to your product that adds value.

Rony: Great brands always stay inside their sector. Let's take the example of Domino's Pizza. They have no branches where they also sell burgers, which is also a very popular food. They stick with selling pizzas. Also Coca-cola, you can see many varieties and apparently they're doing everything, but their core business is beverages and they divide them in 8 categories, but always remain in the same core business.

Dan: But they do concerts, restaurant openings, all their campaigns are about happiness.

Rony: Don't misunderstand their marketing strategies. They sponsor concerts, but don't execute or operate them; they hire companies to do it. Remember: "Mind your own business".

Rony: What's the main problem you solve for your customers?

Dan: I supply them with Thermo sealed packaging with high quality impression. There are only three producers in LATAM. We are one of them and we solve our customers' needs with a package for their products

Rony: Which product adds more value to your customers? Which ones do you have more control over? Which ones give you a higher profitability? Which ones do you like the most?

Dan: Definitely packages. That's the product I can control the most because the manufacturing is just downstairs. I know the key suppliers of the industry and I already have a reputation.

Rony: Great! Once we have eliminated those products that don't have anything to do with your core business from your catalog, it will be easier to operate the company, have cash reserves, be more efficient, and have satisfied customers.

Dan: But Rony, how will I have satisfied customers if I'm not going to provide cleaning products for them or make their web pages anymore?

Rony: Excellent question. You're right, there are some customers that won't be happy, but there are also customers for whom you're not delivering their packages on time because you're distracted with these other products, and they'll start to see that your service will improve.

Remember I told you that the process of change will ache and essential actions have to be taken to have a better company that can grow and stop depending on you. This is one of those aches and fears.

Dan: I can see how doing a little bit of everything and not focusing on what really matters is hurting the company. To be honest, cleaning products and web pages were only opportunities that were presented to me along the way The need I had at the moment and not knowing how to say no led me to incorporate them. I don't really pay attention to them.

Rony: I have a client that learned this lesson the hard way. He has a digital marketing business. His core business is digital reputation, meaning, what people know and say about you in social media and the internet. He was very good at what he did. He was the typical entrepreneur that says yes to every challenge and opportunity. Little by little, opportunities were presented and he said yes to all of them. His agency was known as one of the best agencies of digital reputation, to the point where they could do something not many companies from that industry can, which is to delete information from the internet.

Dan: How can people delete information from the internet?

Rony: I don't exactly know how, but I know that at least the links that carry information can be deleted.

Dan: But is that legal?

Rony: The way they do it, it is. Going back to the story, a while later they agreed to do different things, the marketing agency used to make web pages, SEO, social media, logo design, Scrum lessons, outsourcing of people with programming talent, and even exporting honey to Europe.

Dan: Well, I suppose that while having so many products he could have constant sales and cash flow each month and had many employees handling each one of them.

Rony: No, he didn't. He had around 70 people working and no one coped at all. Customers were constantly complaining, they lived in chaos. He had bad results, too many people and expenses. That's

why he always looked for new sources of income, which ironically were feeding the beast.

Dan: So he was mediocre in many things.

Rony: Yes, I think *it is better to be extraordinary in one thing than mediocre in many.* When I was working with him we figured out which was his core business and little by little we eliminated the products that no longer had anything to do with it.

Dan: So he let all the other opportunities pass?

Rony: Some of them, yes, but he learned a new ability: when his customers present opportunities to him that don't correspond to his core business, he can look for someone who can do it and receive a finder's fee. That way, he won't be distracted with the operations he can't control. Instead he can get many strategic alliances, his customers will be happier and he's going to be seen as a strategic partner not only for his digital reputation, but also because he finds people who can satisfy the needs of his customers.

Dan: I suppose that's why medical specialization exists, where an orthodontist is not the same as a dentist. On one occasion, I took my wife with the orthodontist for a procedure and she asked him while she was there, if he could whiten her teeth. To which he answered that he didn't have the equipment for that kind of procedure. He only dedicates his time to what he knows, and he is a very good orthodontist. I wish I could only focus on what I'm good at!

Rony: We're going to get there. The key is learning to be selective with what we do, for whom we do it, and how we do it. That way, you can become an expert in your industry, your customers will be happier, and you'll have a better reputation and greater competitive advantage against your competition.

Dan: Perfect, that's clear. Core business will help me maintain the attention and focus on the result that I want. It will be challenging, but the perks are worth it. We'll start by eliminating every product and service that isn't part of manufacturing and selling packages. I know some customers will be uncomfortable, but I have to think about

what's best for the company, and I'm sure that being distracted by other activities and products is leading me down the wrong path. I have to keep in mind that when customers ask for other products or services, instead of personally taking advantage of the opportunity, I have to learn how to say no, or find a supplier who can help my customer, even if I don't get a commission for it. The important thing is that I don't get distracted. Connecting my customers with new suppliers will help me strengthen strategic alliances with other companies. The cycle of "if you scratch my back, I'll scratch yours" can begin. It will be challenging, but I know I can make it happen. Most importantly, I have to focus on what's really important and stop chasing butterflies, as you said.

Conclusions:

- Identify the problem you are solving for your customers, then eliminate every distraction (other products or services) and focus on being the best at what you do, making YOUR company an extraordinary supplier.
- Once you understand your core business, you have to evaluate the products, solutions and services that you offer.

10 PRODUCTS THAT ARE PART OF SUCCESS.

> **»** What would happen if you discover that your star product isn't profitable? With each piece you sell, you're losing 10 cents.
>
> **»** It's necessary to make an analysis of the products and solutions that we have in order to discover which ones are part of the recipe for success. Not every product adds value to the results of the organization.

Rony: Have you ever heard about the Pareto principle? The **Pareto or principle**, also known as the 80/20 Rule, establishes that, generally, around 80% of the consequences come from 20% of the causes. Vilfredo Federico Pareto (1848-1923) was an Italian engineer, sociologist, economist and philosopher, whose principle or law can be useful as a reference to focus on what really matters. It can help us have greater satisfaction with less effort and without wasting energy and resources on obtaining poor results. For example, in the business world the Pareto principle is usually used in sales and administration fields. In many cases you can prove that 80% of a company's sales come from 20% of its clients or products, or 80% of the expenses come from 20% of the suppliers. It can also apply in logistics (by controlling 20% of stocked products you can control 80% of the value of the products in your warehouse), or in software engineering (80% of the faults of a software program originate in 20% of that software's code). For the next step, it is important to involve your team so we can make decisions and raise data. We'll make an ABC analysis of products, where we'll understand

which are the 20% of the products that generate 80% of your revenue, profit and other elements. Let's continue simplifying and standardizing your company, so it can be easier to handle.

Dan: How? Now you want me to cut off products?

Rony: Right. We're going to **cut off products.** You'll be surprised by the information we're about to obtain and how you are going to be able to make better decisions. On one occasion, one of my clients that manufactures plastic balls discovered his star product, the one he sold the most of, was making him lose 10 cents per piece; instead of making money he was losing money. When can we meet with your team for at least four hours to make the **ABC analysis of your products?**

Dan: Sometimes I think I'm losing money with some of my products, but I haven't dared to take the risk of doing an analysis.

Rony: The more products you have the more complex is the operation and sales. Human beings need to have options, but not too many. Dan Ariely has made countless experiments to prove what he calls "economical behavior." For example, at a supermarket he placed two beers, one at $2.50 and the other at $1.80. 80% of people bought the most expensive one. When a third beer was placed with the price of $1.60, 80% of people bought the $1.80 beer, 20% bought the $2.50 beer and nobody bought the cheaper one at $1.60. This showed the beer company a price strategy for influencing their customers to buy what they wanted, so from time to time, they stop supplying the $1.60 beer so people will buy the $2.50 one.

Dan: Really? Are we that easily manipulated?

Rony: Yes, we can be influenced by the price or quantity of products. Having too many products at a company is counterproductive. You should have a warehouse to store your raw material and finished product. Your sales team needs to know all the variety of products that you have and probably carry a bag with many samples to show to new customers.

Dan: Oh, and also the number of specification manuals and that my staff should be prepared for all the variants. Training is a huge investment.

Rony: Through time, you were the one who adapted to the needs of your clients, which makes sense. But now, since your company is stable, it is better for you to start establishing the rules of engagement, so now your clients can adapt to you; that way, you'll be more efficient at satisfying their needs.

Dan: That would be great! There are products that are a nightmare and the clients who buy them are even worse. Adjusting the production line for changes in production, besides being dangerous, is very expensive. If what you suggest will make our production runs longer, it will definitely make us more efficient and profitable.

Rony: That's the idea. Standardizing and simplifying the operation will make your company more profitable. Cutting off products is part of the process.

Dan: I understand the concept, but to be honest, I fear the competition because they have a wider variety of products than we do, and I wouldn't like to be left behind.

Rony: Is having more variety of products giving them a competitive advantage?

Dan: I don't think so, but they certainly have more variety.

Rony: I understand that you want to have more SKUs than the competition, but you're fighting the wrong battle. The battle you have to win is called efficiency. If you are more efficient than your competition, you'll have a better reputation, service and profitability, and thereby, you'll have more possibilities to "survive" the competition. "Less is more." I suggest we make an analysis. Don't jump to conclusions until you have the numbers in front of you.

Dan: Agreed. We can meet next Tuesday morning, as long as your agenda is free.

Rony: Perfect. We'll see each other on Tuesday at your office. Please explain the Pareto principle to your team. For the meeting, I need your team to prepare the following **information per product:**

❭ Updated costs

❭ Selling price

- Volume record
- Selling cycles
- Inventory occupation percentage
- Manufacture complexity
- Manufacture time
- Quantity of customers that require the product
- Other details that are important to consider

Tuesday morning arrived. It was a rainy and cold day. Everyone gathered at the meeting room with coffee, cookies and Dan had his green juice, which he drinks every morning.

Rony: Thanks to everyone for being here. We're going to assemble the information and make decisions that will help make the company more efficient and easier to handle. I would like to know if Dan had the opportunity to share the information of the core business update and the Pareto principle with you.

Carlos: Yes, he explained the Pareto principle. I thought it was interesting. I never realized that this pattern could be repeated.

Victor: But it doesn't happen all the time.

Dan: I believe that's why they call it Pareto principle and not Pareto law. The law of gravity always applies, there are no exceptions.

Diana: See? 100% of Dan's comments are either illustrative or educational.

Ha ha ha, we all laughed.

Rony: Ok, so you understood the 80/20 Rule. And what about core business?

Alex: When Dan explained the concept and told us our core business is manufacturing packages and that we'll keep doing that, cutting off little by little what doesn't have to do with it, I almost cried of joy. The other two businesses: selling cleaning products and creating web pages, caused many administrative problems, and worse, I always found out they weren't profitable.

Carlos: I'm not totally convinced yet. We have to give customers what they want.

Dan: Precisely because we've been thinking like that nowadays we have many products, customers and complaints. We're not excellent at anything. We're mediocre at everything, and that's not what I want. I don't want to only brag about our revenue, I want to brag about the great company that we are, so that we can become irreplaceable.

Rony: Carlos, I understand your doubt and discomfort. It's time for you to learn how to say NO. And that's why we're here, because we're going to take the word NO to the next level. Not every product that you have contributes to the company's growth. Some of them can even be counterproductive for general results.

Victor: Finally! My prayers were listened to! I hope we can eliminate SKU 4098. For years it has been a headache. Only one customer buys it and he always complains and is late on his payments. To make things more complicated, it occupies a lot of space in the warehouse and the raw material suppliers are about to go out of business. Really, each time I see it on the production plan I want to cry out of frustration. But we carry it forward, as we do with everything at the company.

Rony: I can't commit to eliminating SKU 4098, but we'll definitely analyze many components you mentioned that make a product attractive for the company.

Diana: A while ago I heard that General Electric, under Jack Welch's leadership, decided to be number 1 or 2 in each industry they competed in, which led them to eliminate many divisions of their company and also many products. Before, they had a plastics division with products like Lexan and Plexiglas, which were very successful; nevertheless, GE lost competitive advantage and their leadership in the plastics industry, to the point where the division stopped being profitable, so he decided to sell that division to a company that would be happy with the profit margin that for GE wasn't ideal. They have eliminated many divisions and products.

Carlos: Ok, but you are talking about GE. They have many resources and they can afford to eliminate products or divisions.

Rony: We can't afford not to be efficient. Later, when you have the complete analysis you can make a decision, but for now, I ask you to have an open mind for this exercise so we can find solutions that would benefit the company. Remember: "what's best for the company." You already have some information we can use to start making the ABC analysis of products. I'm sure you'll want to include more categories that will help us have a wider vision.

Alex: I would like to tell you that updating product costs was quite an adventure. They hadn't been updated for a very long time, and I was surprised because some products aren't profitable anymore, and we can't continue selling them at the same price that we sell them today. I already presented the results to Dan.

Carlos: It is impossible to raise our prices. We even have to find a way to give our customers discounts so they could buy a larger volume.

Dan: What? Are you willing to keep selling a product that is not profitable? Even worse, that's making us lose more money? That's something I'm not willing to do. Every deal we've made with our customers has been with the "win-win" mindset. It's not about them winning and us losing.

Rony: I'm glad you changed your mind.

Dan: Yes, I have noticed my way of thinking has been changing throughout this process. Before, it made sense to sell anything at any price only to survive, but luckily, we're no longer in that situation; we are a growing, stable company. You said to me, "We shall create new habits that will make us better." We can't keep doing the same thing and expect different results.

Diana: I think Einstein said that, right?

Dan: Yes, it's very accurate for this moment.

Rony: **ABC analysis** is a statistical study that helps categorize products according to their relevance: **Type A articles:** the most important, most used or sold; as well as the ones that generate more

revenue and profit. **Type B articles:** these have secondary importance, so the revenue and profit are less than Type A articles. **Type C articles:** the least important, provides the least benefit, can even generate expenses.

Victor: I know that methodology, it's very common for analyzing stock inventory and rotation.

Rony: Exactly, it's the same one. We only added some elements that will help us understand which products contribute to the results of the organization and which don't. At the end we'll see something like this:

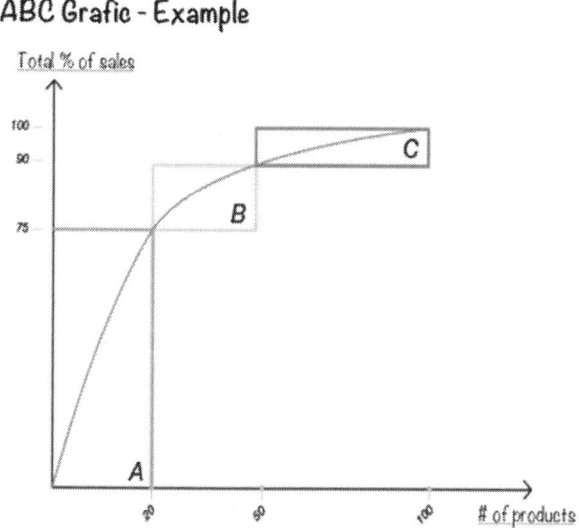

Rony: Together we built the basis of ABC product analysis, where we discovered that from 60 SKUs that the company has nowadays, 20 have to be eliminated because they aren't helping the company. They are just satisfying specific needs of some customer without giving a real benefit to your company.

Dan: Now I have a clearer and wider vision. I understood which products are counterproductive and that even if they're our "little babies", we have to eliminate them. C products are playing against us and what Victor always said now was confirmed: SKU 4098 is a type

C product, so we have to cut it off for the sake of the company. Carlos, I know you don't agree because you represent the Sales team and you care about the interests of the customers, but let's remember that you are part of this team. As we learned in the five dysfunctions of a team, I'm going to ask for your commitment and fulfilment with the decisions we make, which I want to review so we don't forget anything.

Action plan format.

Carlos: Prepare a notice letter for the customers about the discontinuation of products. May 13th.

Carlos: Meet with customers that are affected by the discontinuation of products to try to find an alternative or sell them other products. May 30th.

Alex: Notify suppliers about our discontinuation of products seeking to maintain savings with the rest of our raw materials. May 22nd.

Victor: Make an inventory of C products raw material, quantifying the finished product and calculate how much raw material is required to comply with our commitments for the next three months. May 20th.

Diana: Train the staff of the company about the core business and ABC analysis. June 1st.

Dan: I love that I don't have to do everything anymore. Tasks are starting to be delegated. This exercise we did together helped strengthen our team and also ensure the continuity and a healthy evolution of the company.

Conclusions:

- Having fewer and profitable products also makes the company profitable, efficient and standardized.

- It's not only necessary to identify key products, but also the customers who can take you to the next level.

 **CLIENT CATEGORY.**

> ❭ The recipe for failure is very simple: trying to satisfy everyone.
>
> ❭ We have to focus on the efforts and resources of the company to make our ideal customers happy, those who we really want to work with, instead of doing a poor job of satisfying every customer.

Rony: While companies are growing and developing they **gain customers,** either by recommendation of other customers, by the effort of the sales team, or by the promotion they do. When we have a new customer we're so happy to welcome them, we don't worry if they want to change our products, ask for different prices or payment conditions. We agree to almost everything to satisfy every customer because we want to have a higher income.

Dan: Yes, as it should be.

Rony: Not really. Satisfying everyone is actually the perfect recipe for exponential chaos, and eventually, organizational failure.

Dan: Don't tell me that now you're going to ask me to end relations with some of my customers. Don't you see we don't have enough cash flow and we've had a bad reputation in the market because of our deliveries?

Rony: That's precisely my point. Don't you see that your cash flow problem is because of the non-compliance of payment from your customers? Do you have a lot of money tied up in inventory because of the diversity and variety of the products you have per customer?

Your bad reputation of late deliveries on the market is related to the fact that most of your customers don't comply with the minimum requirements of delivery, whether it's the truck capacity, unloading platform, etc., which complicates logistics. Clearly, you don't have a logistics company, because you're not good at it. We already talked about it in our last meeting. You're wonderful at making packages, so we have to find a way to simplify everything that's not related to that. Having many customers is not an indicator of success. Can you tell me if every customer is satisfied? Paying on time? Do they recommend you to other prospects? Do you have fun working with them? Do you seek to grow by their side? Do you trust them?

Dan: Mmn, actually, no. Only a few customers can comply with what you're mentioning. But if I only worked with those customers, I would have less income and I would have to fire people.

Rony: To have satisfied customers that pay on time and recommend you to others is an indicator of success. Having customers that you have fun with, that you seek to grow with them and trust them is also an indicator of success. Right now we're only going to analyze your customers. Later on we'll see who you want to keep, and finally, we'll make an exit plan for the customers you no longer want to keep. You may have to fire some people because you probably have more people than you need. **Having temporary solutions for permanent problems is not right**. Do you remember the soldiers that were compensating for the weight of the log? Having more employees doesn't make you more successful.

Dan: I don't totally agree with that.

Rony: I understand, your resistance is normal, it's even healthy. If money wasn't a restriction, are there some customers you want to "fire"?

Dan: Well, putting it that way, yes. There are some customers that are a nightmare. They ask for low volume below minimum requirements. They ask for many changes, and it takes them forever to pay. I have a customer in Florida who has an average capacity, but in every delivery he complains about something and he always has excuses not to pay. Picture this: one time he called me on my mobile in the middle of a

family dinner to yell at me because the driver of the truck wasn't wearing the company's uniform, and he told me he couldn't be sure it was really us who were delivering. Every month he uses a different excuse not to pay us. He says his customers didn't pay him, or that he had to increase the salary of his staff, or that he's on an audit. The worst was one time he told me he couldn't fulfill my payment because he went on a family vacation to Italy for 2 weeks and he didn't have money, but he demanded we send a new container with his packages. Anyway, I don't like him at all.

Rony: As you can see, we're talking about the same situation here. That situation that clouds your judgment and decision making is cash flow. This is caused, among other things, by the customers you had to fire a long time ago. As you can see, you're living in a vicious cycle because you have many customers but only a few of them are ideal or core customers. You think you should have to make them happy so they can keep you busy. You're distracted dealing with complicated, defaulting, conflictive customers.

Dan: Ok, if you have the solution to eliminate nightmarish customers and make more money I'm all ears.

Rony: More than ears, I want you to be more ready to set your decision making in motion. We have already walked a few steps to achieve this, now we have to continue classifying customers. We'll use the 80/20 Pareto principle to identify who is your ideal customer, and a similar exercise to the ABC analysis of products. After that, with that reduced group of customers, we'll go deeper to understand who they are, what they're looking for, etc,. to make a Buyer Persona. Once we have a complete picture, without pressure from my side, you'll make decisions about who are the customers that you still want to work with, how we are going to fire inappropriate customers, and how are we going to attract new customers that you DO want to have.

Dan: I'm excited, I like the idea. But I can't deny I am also afraid.

Rony: Fear is a good indicator. It means we're doing something different. Fear is a good advisor but a bad influence if it doesn't let you move forward.

Dan: I suppose we have to work through this with my team. Does next Thursday at the office meeting room work for you? What do we need to work on before?

Rony: Yes, that works for me. You have to bring a database of your customers, your purchases, how frequently they order, and the number and type of complaints. Bring all the numbers you have from your customers. See you next week. Enjoy your weekend.

The next week, on Thursday morning, the team arrived on time at the meeting room. They were enthusiastic because of the things we were going to work on, and also nervous because they knew we always made decisions of great impact.

Dan: I appreciate everyone arriving on time and that you're cooperating with this process of organizational change. Rony, I want to tell you that making the database of the customers was a very difficult task. We weren't clear about how many customers we had, and we didn't have a consolidated database, which made this task a little long and difficult.

Rony: Well, congratulations for being able to organize the information. Now we can use it to make some progress. Can I see the database?

Victor proudly presented the Excel matrix of customers. It had the total of sales, units, SKUs quantity, frequency of purchases, among other elements.

Rony: Team, I'm going to ask you to add new factors to evaluate customers. Some of the points won't have hard data or numbers to evaluate, but will have an emotion, which is also valid, but let's measure preferably with numbers. I want to add profit, recommendations (if this customer recommended us to other customers), on-time payment, complexity of manufacture. Can you come up with some others?

Diana raised her hand excitedly and said: Fun! It's fun to work with them.

Everyone was happy with Diana's contribution, who is usually reserved. They thought her idea was very accurate.

Rony: Before we start to evaluate, I would like to share some stories with you to clarify something that will help us understand this

exercise. A bride and groom are organizing their wedding. They have 350 invitees. How many people have to be happy at the wedding? At least two, the bride and groom. It is very common that at weddings people complain about everything, the location, the time, the color of flowers, the food, the drinks, the music and many other things. A wedding is successful when the bride and groom are happy. If they're happy probably the guests are too. But if the bride and groom try to satisfy the needs and complaints of each and every one of their guests, we'll have two slaves and 348 people presenting complaints.

Victor: I suppose that's why restaurants have a sign that says, "We reserve the right to refuse admission." And rightly so. If I'm eating at a family restaurant with my kids and suddenly a group of young people arrive drunk, making noise, singing and smoking like the restaurant was a bar, my experience turns into something unpleasant, and I won't go back to that restaurant.

Rony: I always try to travel with Southwest Airlines because it has a young, simple, practical, casual and fun style, and it's not expensive. It has acceptable prices, good flight frequency, many destinations, and a kind staff. When I travel with Southwest Airlines, I feel different. The flight attendants or customer service agents always treat me with respect and almost every time with a smile on their faces.

Alex: Just like Volaris, a Mexican company! Oh! They're really awful. They're always in a bad mood. Their flights are cheap but there is always something extra you have to pay for. I try not to travel with them not only for their bad service, but because they trick people. The last time I travelled with my children, the front desk agent decided nobody could board the plane with food. At the beginning I didn't question him, but once we were on board everything, and I mean EVERYTHING had an extra charge. Suddenly, I saw one of my kids sweating and suffering, so I asked him what was happening. He said he really needed to go to the bathroom, but he didn't want to pay.

Ha ha ha, everyone laughed and felt sorry for the kid.

Rony: Volaris is a bad copy of Southwest. They tried to copy their business model without success. I remember once I was traveling

on Southwest on a Boeing 737, and I heard flight attendants having fun during the process of security instructions. The guy from the microphone turned the moment of sharing security information into a stand-up comedy, which resulted in a very funny experience to what is generally boring one, or we don't even pay attention. That happens frequently on Southwest flights.

Rony: Nevertheless, it turns out that not everyone appreciates humor like I do. I'm going to share a well-known story in the business world. It's about knowing your ideal core customer and letting go of those who aren't. A customer took extreme actions to inform Southwest of her disapproval. A woman who frequently flew with Southwest was constantly disappointed about every aspect of the company's operation. In fact, she was known as Mrs. Complaints, because after every flight she filed a complaint. She didn't like the fact that the company didn't assign seats; she didn't like the absence of a first class section; she didn't like not having food on board; she didn't like Southwest's boarding procedure; she didn't like the flight attendants sport uniforms and the unconventional environment; she didn't like the jokes the staff made about security instructions, she explained the importance security had for her and the crew, and that it was a lack of respect for her and the crew that the staff was singing or making jokes before they took off. Her last letter was a litany of complaints, which baffled the Customer Service agents, who decided to address the case to Herb Kelleher, the CEO of the company, with a note that said, "This is for you". In 60 seconds Kelleher replied and said: "Dear Mrs. Crabapple: We'll miss you. Love, Herb". He even posted it in the newspaper.

Dan: For real? The CEO did that? What a nerve!

Rony: Yes, why wouldn't he? You wouldn't let someone in your house who treats your family badly, complains about food, complains about x y z.

Dan: You're right, but I can't deny the entry to my mother-in-law. Ha ha ha, everyone laughed.

Rony: Southwest Airlines' ideal customer is an executive of a Start-up or medium company, around 30 or 40 years old, who travels a lot,

has a family at home and a limited budget. The company decided to satisfy that kind of customer and make him happy to the point where the three promises of the brand are 3 L's: Lots of fun, Lots of flights and Low prices. They know their ideal customer.

Alex: It makes sense: if I try to satisfy everyone who pays, I won't make anyone happy. Nevertheless, if we have enough ideal customers and they're happy, they'll bring similar customers.

We spent hours evaluating and discussing point by point to reach an evaluation and find our "top 10 customers".

Dan: Finally I understand who is our core customer. To be honest, I thought keeping our Florida customer was very important because he's one of our biggest customers, but now I realize he's not that big, he was only loud enough to be on my mind all the time.

Rony: I'm glad you noticed that. Now that we have reached this point, do you remember I told you that you can't make everyone happy, but only a little group of people? Well, that group is your **"Top 10,"** whom you have to make EXTRA HAPPY. Do you remember the story of the bride and groom? Well, the same happens here: let's make those 10 customers happy, listen to their ideas, suggestions and recommendations, and they will help you escalate correctly. Now imagine we can attract more customers with those characteristics.

Dan: It would be great! If we attract more customers like the "Top 10" we can escalate correctly, with forecasts and profit. Now I understand what you were saying before: this can help us be more efficient, standardized and simplified. Our other 60 customers generate lots of problems on different levels and areas of the company. It's a pity these "Top 10" customers don't generate enough income to fire the other 60.

Rony: Right, but with a plan to attract "Top 10" customers we'll generate more income. Nevertheless, of the 60 customers you have now, there are some that shouldn't be working with you anymore; for starters, those who aren't profitable, who don't pay on time or treat your employees badly.

Dan: But how can I eliminate those customers without being rude? Telling them I won't be providing my services anymore sounds very rude, I don't want to burn my reputation on the market.

Rony: For starters, you have every right to tell a customer you don't want to provide your services anymore, but if you want to make it more political, you can write a memo where you write all the new sales restrictions, new standards that the "Top 10" customers fulfill and the rest don't. That way, those who aren't willing to meet those requirements will decide not to work with you anymore. So they'll be making the decision.

Dan: Ok. So the commercial team and I have the assignment of making a plan for customers who will no longer serve and also a communication plan where we explain our new sales conditions. If they don't accept them, they'll be making their decision.

Rony: To increase the "Top 10", we should generate our Buyer Persona model. The Buyer Persona model is a semi-fictional representation of our final (or potential) consumer, built from demographic information, behavior, needs and motivations. It's about standing in the shoes of our Core ideal customers to understand what they need from us. We'll have a better understanding of the ideal customer, his fears, desires, needs, tastes and more.

Carlos: I'm a bit familiar with the Buyer Persona model, also known as ideal customer. When I arrived at the company, we did an initial exercise and made a draft, but we never used it. I don't know where I left it.

Rony: I think we have enough information with the Excel document and the graphic. Besides, the information from your draft might be different now.

Dan: If you find it, it would be helpful if you could compare the result of that previous exercise with the result we'll get today.

Rony: What are the similar characteristics among your "Top 10" customers?

Diana: Almost all of them are men and founders of their companies.

Carlos: Most of them use our products to pack theirs, which is a personal care product. Moreover, their products are sold to big supermarket chains.

Dan: I know all of them personally. They're people I feel comfortable having lunch with; our conversations are very interesting.

Alex: I don't know if this adds value, but almost all of their leaders of the department of accounts receivables are women.

Rony: Everything adds value. In the end, we want to have the complete picture. What else?

Victor: We have a long-term production plan with their particular needs. It's very unusual that we change their production program.

As the meeting went on, we found the resemblance among "Top 10" customers.

Rony: Perfect, now we have something clearer. Now's the time for us to deeply understand the profile of these "Top 10" customers. When they hire your services or buy your products; what are their fears, desires and needs?

There was silence in the room for a few minutes. Everyone grabbed their notebooks and individually wrote their ideas in order to share them with the group later. After brainstorming, categorizing and cleaning, the final result was:

Our ideal customer's name is Marcos. He is between 35 and 44 years old, he's an entrepreneur and the founder of his company. He's married with 2.5 kids, his level of education is a degree in Administration. He likes to travel to Las Vegas once a year to the CES convention in January. He loves technological developments. He likes to read Isaac Asimov, Salim Ismail and Dan Ariely's books. He sells products and articles of personal care, especially skin care. His customers are international supermarket chains like Wal-Mart. His desire is to have confidence that our deliveries will be proper and on time. His fear is that the quality and impression of our products are below his expectations because our package is the first look people give to his product.

Victor: Compared with the previous exercise, they are similar but this one is much more complete. With this exercise we can hire a digital marketing agency and ask them to find prospects with these characteristics. That service is named "lead generation" and to do it, almost every time they ask for that information. It was good we did this together!

Dan: I had never had the concept of my customer as clearly as I have now. Even knowing his tastes and reading preferences will help me a lot, because now I know what we can talk about. I think I'll watch movies like Will Smith's "*I, robot*", which is based on Asimov's book to have more things to talk about.

Alex: That's good because your connection will be deeper. It would be like doing business with friends.

Rony: That's the idea. From now on, instead of letting the wind decide our direction, **we'll be the ones who decide in which direction the company will go.** We're **designing** the future of the organization.

Dan: We can't afford to lose any of the "Top 10" customers, any "Marcos". We have to attract more customers like him and eliminate customers like the one from Florida.

Rony: Is it much more expensive bringing new customers than keeping old ones.

Diana: Wait, I didn't understand that, can you explain it a little more?

Rony: Yes. To attract a new customer you make lots of efforts, visits, reunions, proposals, quotations. It's a long and expensive process. But when you have repeat customers that buy your products frequently, it is much easier and economical to work with them.

Victor: That's true. The process of getting a new customer can last months and many meetings: emails coming and going without reaching anything; meanwhile, with the customers that we regularly work with, we only have to follow up their needs and re-stock.

Alex: I have mixed feelings. I understand the logic of having more "Top 10" customers or "Marcos" and eliminating "nightmare

customers", as Dan says, but that wouldn't be some kind of racism or classism?

Dan: I propose we change "nightmare customer" for "Below 10", so we can have more clarity about who our "**Top 10 and Below 10**" customers are.

Rony: Answering Alex's question, as you should know, airlines and other companies have a VIP program for their regular customers. Like American Airlines, which has four levels of their AAdvantage elite program, and each level has different benefits. Or American Express, their VIP customers have Black credit cards which are only given to a reduced group of people by invitation; Amazon, their Amazon Prime program, which gives extra benefits to customers. As you can see, companies are starting to see the strength behind knowing their "Top 10" customers and finding the way to make them as happy as possible, because they know they'll attract similar customers.

Dan: I love that! If our "Top 10" customers bring new customers, I'll stop investing in marketing and start investing in paying for their lunches and giving them science fiction books. They will generate the reputation and marketing that we need.

As minutes passed the team was more enthusiastic, writing down plans to give more satisfaction to "Top 10" customers and to attract more "Marcos".

Rony: It's important to make a customer satisfaction questionnaire for the "Top 10", to have more clarity about what we do right, what we do wrong, and what we can do better.

Carlos: Yes, I already have a questionnaire we send each quarter.

Rony: How many people answer it?

Carlos 7% (said proudly).

Rony: That number is extremely low. It's not enough to make decisions or evaluations. Can you show us that questionnaire?

On the screen we saw a 12-question questionnaire projected, which had a lot of information.

Rony: Remember Marcos's characteristics, he's your ideal customer: busy man, with a family and a company to run. Does someone understand why you only get 7% of the answers?

Dan: I wouldn't answer that, it's very long. It seems it takes a lot of time answering it.

Rony: You hit the nail on the head. It takes a lot of the customer's time and that's why he's not cooperating. Some years ago, Fred Reichheld created a methodology named NPS, a tool that measures the loyalty and satisfaction of the customer. His first reference appeared in 2003, in an article with the title "The One Number You Need To Grow", written by Reichheld and published by the Harvard Business Review. He only asked one question: *How likely is it that you would recommend [company X] to a friend or colleague?*

Dan: If that were the only question of course I'd answer it. It wouldn't take me long.

Rony: What I suggest is that we add a second question: "Why?" We would have deeper information and the answer would be entirely from the customer. So the customer receives only one question with the follow up: "From 0 to 10, how likely is it that you recommend our products or services? Why?".

Carlos: That sounds simple, two answers from the customer will help us analyze results better and we would have more answers than we have today, but I think we're going to fall short on information.

Dan: If we get 70% of the answers with only 2 questions, we'll have more information than we have today with 7% answers of 12 questions.

Alex: And how can we **quantify results**? Sorry, I'm much for numbers and I think that having tangible, objective information we can plot, will help us make better decisions.

Rony: That's the beauty of this model. To answer NPS, they only have to select a number from 0 to 10.

Alex: Perfect! And that will give us an average.

Rony: We won't have an average. Fred's methodology is calculated differently. He considers those who answer from 0 to 6 as detractors, 7 to 8 as neutral, and 9 to 10 as promoters. Detractors are those who criticize the company, neutrals are those who don't care about it and who don't have loyalty towards it, promoters are those who, as their name says,

promote the company and enhance its reputation. There's an online calculator that gives you the results according to this methodology: http://www.npscalculator.com/en

Victor: I just found the calculator and I can see types of people divided by traffic light colors. Detractors as red, neutral as yellow and promoters as green. Once again, we can see the impact of the use of these colors. I love it.

Rony: To give you an idea of how much this methodology is used around you, and you haven't even noticed, I'll tell you this: each time you go to Wal-Mart, to some bank, public bathrooms at malls, etc; there's a little screen that says: "How satisfied are you with our service?" It has three faces, one red, one yellow and one green. Even on YouTube from now on it appears a sign for you to grade your experience with a series of little faces. All these examples are based on the same methodology.

Dan: I can't believe it, you're right. To be honest, each time someone isn't friendly, I click on the red face many times.

Victor: That's how you demonstrate your anger towards the waitress who treated you badly? That's being passive-aggressive.

Ha ha ha, we all laughed.

Dan: Yes, I'm guilty of grading only when the service is bad; I have to make a habit of grading also when it's good.

Diana: I think we should all apply that habit. Recognizing and seeing the positive side is something we all have to do more often, starting by recognizing the good things that the staff of the company does, not only calling their attention when they do something wrong.

Rony: Those are excellent points of view. I promise when we work on employees' life cycles, we'll talk about the importance of acknowledgement.

Dan: So, let's add to the action plan the design and sending out the new questionnaire; Carlos, please take care of that.

Rony: To conclude the customer's issue, I would like to share something about customer service and customer experience. I'll start by quoting the following phrase: "At the end of the day, people won't remember what you said or did. They'll remember how you made them feel," Maya Angelou. Customers are smarter than ever. They know what it is to have a good customer service experience. Brands like Apple, Amazon and Zappos have shown us over and over again. Your customers aren't comparing you with your competition anymore, they're comparing you with any other company that gives them a memorable experience, and when you fail them, they'll ask themselves why you can't be as good as those companies.

Dan: But we aren't competing with Amazon or its products.

Victor: But people use those services and inevitably compare us with them.

Rony: Customer service is the assistance given to customers before, during and after buying or using a product or service. Brands make an effort to improve customer satisfaction and loyalty, so they can create long lasting relationships. It's a reactive activity. Customer experience is the sum of every interaction a customer has with the company. According to Forrester, customer experience (CX) is defined

as: "How customers perceive their interactions with your company." It's a proactive activity.

Examples of the difference between customer experience and customer service:

Customer service	Customer experience
How kind the staff is and how fast they bring the food.	The cleanliness of the restaurant, the taste/quality of the food, the variety of options on the menu, the environment, the prices and where they can sit while eating there.
How well a store's agent answers the questions of a customer.	The ease of walking around a store, the availability of products, variety of available options and payment rate.
How fast customer problems are solved.	Why the customer had a problem or a question since the beginning, and how frequently a customer has problems with the company.

Dan: We are very reactive. We've focused on addressing our customers correctly when they have a complaint or when they call us, but we haven't implemented any way to make their experience memorable while they interact with us, and that's customer experience. From now on, we'll focus our efforts on making our "Top 10" customers happy so they can recommend us.

Carlos: I'll start searching for more customers with these characteristics. Our "Marcos" is very illustrative. If we reduce our "Below 10" customers and increase our "Top 10" customers, the complaints will decrease.

Diana: I feel that having more "Top 10" customers will make our company more profitable, effective and happier. I think there would be less drama and Dan would be more relaxed.

Dan: A toast to Diana's observation.

Conclusions:

- ❿ Classifying your customers will help you identify your group of ideal customers. This step alone is huge, making the transaction of eliminating "Below 10" customers and attracting more ideal or "Top 10" customers, will make the company more standardized, predictable and profitable.

- ❿ To achieve having a more selected and more satisfied group of customers, you should have a group of employees that meet the expectations of your customers.

12 EMPLOYEE LIFECYCLE.

> The Rolling Stones sing in one of their songs: "You can't always get what you want... You get what you need."
>
> Every company has something in common, employees; payroll is generally what absorbs a big part of the monthly budget. Employees shape the culture of the company, a sense of community working towards the same purpose. But that doesn't happen spontaneously; there should be a plan designed and executed.

Rony: How are you feeling with the progress we've made?

Dan: Very good, it has been an eye opener. This process has really revealed information that I hadn't had the opportunity to understand, and it has helped me see the impact of some of my decisions and the reality I lived in. It has changed my perspective. I haven't discovered something I wasn't aware of, but your process has forced me to clarify things and make decisions that help me have control over the company and my life. In fact, my wife has noticed this change and she's very happy that I'm working with you. She wants to invite you and your wife to have dinner at our house on the last Thursday of the month. Could you join us?

Rony: Of course, we'll be happy to. What can we bring?

Dan: A bottle of wine would be ok.

Rony: Perfect! In the meantime, let's get to work. This is one of the pillars that you control the most to make decisions, and it will possibly be the most painful: **employees.** When the company is small: between two and 15 employees, all of them were recruited and hired by you; they're people you personally know and who are aligned with you. They trust you and are loyal. But beyond having 15 employees, you need a person who helps you with the hiring process, and while your company grows, you'll be surprised at how many people you don't know who are working for you. Over time, you realize that the types of people, their attitudes and values may or may not be aligned with you, which generates a strange feeling of not knowing the company and not having control over it. If things don't set the course, it gets worse. Drama starts arising at the company; from time to time there are fist fights between employees; the water cooler talks dominate the communication of the company, personal relationships such as couples start to be developed, and the list goes on and on. It becomes a strange place for you.

Dan: Wow, it seems like you've been living at the company; but you were mistaken about one thing. The HR person that I hired to start the employee's process began at the company when I had 20 employees and I couldn't handle the requirements and demands related to the staff. It was too much to do the interviews, assessments, files, worry about the payroll calculation and many other things. That's when I hired Diana, and she has helped me take a lot of the daily operation load related to the staff, but new problems also began.

Rony: That's normal. Did you ever give Diana a manual of how to recruit, hire, introduce, develop, motivate, retire and/or fire your staff?

Dan: No, not at all, that's her job.

Rony: Yes, that's her job, but based on what? Where is the guide to do it?

Dan: By the way, there are lots of activities I didn't understand that were her responsibility. I just hired her to handle the hiring process and the payroll; but eventually, she started helping me also with the firing issue.

Rony: Yes, all those activities I mentioned are known as "employee cycle," which goes from attracting new talents to when someone leaves the company. It's easier if we have a recipe that can be repeated over and over again.

Dan: Recipe?

Rony: Sure! Like a chef who has the recipe to make pecan pie over and over again and almost every time it turns out the same because he repeats the same process and recipe. The same happens at Human Resources. We shall have a recipe for each one of the steps or your efforts won't succeed in the future. Besides, it is better to design the type of culture that you want to have instead of dealing with what was created by your staff. For example, there's a bar in California named Happy sunshine. It had happy, young, and generally blond employees; the owner hired someone to handle the Human Resources area, a girl with "punk" style, so she started hiring people like her. So, little by little the bar started to have employees with tattoos, dark shadows on their eyelids, dark hair, dressed completely in dark and wearing dark chokers. So the owner of Happy sunshine let the company turn into the *Twilight saga*, which neither he nor his customers liked.

Dan: Poor guy, he lost control over his company and it transformed into something different. Tell me at least his company was profitable.

Rony: Yes it was, that bar was always successful, but it wasn't a bar where the owner liked to be or take care of because he didn't identify with it. So he sold it and re-created Happy sunshine at another location; only this time he dedicated time to have a "recipe" or guideline for the "employee cycle".

Dan: I get your point and agree with it. We should find a simpler way to attract and keep talented people.

Rony: Now that you mention talent, do you have any idea of the cost of staff turnover?

Dan: No idea, I would like to think it's their termination payment.

Rony: It's very expensive because you have to select candidates, train them, deal with the mistakes they make in their learning curve and

with their exit; all of that plus the moral damage that a company suffers when people are getting fired constantly. Dr. Brand Smart, author of Topgrading, said the estimated cost of a bad hire ranged between five and 27 times the basic salary of a person. Using the investigation of more than 50 companies, I can tell you that the average cost of a badly hired manager who earns $33 kUSD a year ($2,800 USD a month) is $490,909 USD; 15 times their basic salary. As you can see, financially, it is very expensive not to hire the right people and as I said before, it harms the company not only financially but also the staff's morale.

Dan: 15 times the salary for one bad hire? Wow! That's a lot. I never understood the impact of people coming and going. I was only hiring people when I needed to cover a position as soon as possible to satisfy my customers.

Rony: Of course, that's a normal habit of a Start-up, but right now you have to think differently; you have to operate with the philosophy "hire slow, fire fast".

Dan: Yes, I have heard that phrase a couple of times with some of my friends who are also CEOs of their companies. But to be honest, I thought they were crazy. Sincerely, it's impossible to hire slow, we are always in a hurry to onboard new talent.

Rony: Well, that's something we have to stop doing and start making a process that allows you to attract and filter people accurately. Attracting people is not only posting the opening on job opportunities sites online. You also have to generate organizational culture, a reputation outside the office. Reputation is what will help you have more of the right people knocking at your door. Employees are part of the solution to bring people with talent. So, we have to create an environment at the company where employees feel proud of where they work.

Dan: We can apply NPS to employees so we can measure their satisfaction and correct what needs to be corrected.

Rony: You are a genius! In fact, that is already portrayed in the next part of the NPS methodology, it's called **ENPS, Employee Net Promoter Score,** which is based on the same principles.

Dan: Right now, Diana only applies exit interviews which gives us an idea of what's working or not working at the company. But I don't know how much I can trust that information, because there's not much to do, only be reactive. We can't anticipate anything or be proactive. With ENPS I think we can gather enough information to be proactive and build a workplace where employees feel worthy, proud and can become brand "promoters."

Rony: Definitely. If employees are those who attract talent, your hiring and selecting process will be easier. Even more economical than all the expenses you have today. We also have to define your core values, which means, the type of attitude you want these people to have.

Dan: Did you mean aptitude?

Rony: No, you heard correctly, I said "attitude." Until now you have hired people based on their aptitude, their technical abilities to develop a particular task, but we also have to measure their attitude. What's it worth to have an excellent financial strategist if you don't trust him? Why do you want to have the best salesman of the industry if you fear he will steal from your customers or even from you? I would say that attitude should be 80 and aptitude 20. Obviously, when you seek people for a position it's optimal they have the right aptitude (ability) to develop that job position, at least the foundations. That will help you save time.

Dan: Now I think you're a little crazy, but I'm willing to listen. There have been a few times you have proved me wrong.

Rony: You're not wrong, it's just that no one taught you this and you solved your problems the best you could. You can teach anyone to operate a very difficult piece of machinery without having knowledge about the machine, right? Or does every single one of your machine operators know how to handle your machines when you hire them?

Dan: No, they didn't. Only those who we stole from the competition knew how to operate the machines; we trained the rest here.

Rony: What can you tell me about the people who work in the administration department? I'm sure you spent the right amount of time teaching them how to handle the administration and accounting

of the company. Obviously, it's easier if they have the basic knowledge so you don't have to start from scratch. So, you can teach anyone the aptitudes/abilities of your daily activities, but it's very hard teaching attitudes; meaning, values, ways of acting, how to behave. More precisely, you can't teach anyone to be punctual, optimistic, honorable, loyal, etc. Attitudes or values are the 80% that I just mentioned. Do you have an example of an employee you would like to clone? Someone that arrived without knowing ANYTHING from the company and learned with time, that their vibe and "way of acting and behaving" with their colleagues inside and outside the company is ideal?

Dan: Yes, his name is Eric. He's an amazing person, everyone loves him. He's a good guy and a role model. He started with a great attitude, without knowing anything about the industry. We taught him everything and now he's a role model.

Rony: Do you have an example of someone highly efficient, who has very good aptitudes/abilities, but who you don't trust?

Dan: Yes, his name is Elias. He's a salesman who has been highly efficient over the years. He always reaches his goals, but his ways of doing it concern me. He has lied to the people at the warehouse. I think he even had an affair with the procurement manager of one of our best customers. But I have to admit he gives very good results.

Rony: At what price? Reaching goals without caring who gets hurt along the way, including the name and reputation of the company? These people are known as "wolves in sheep's clothing." They are very dangerous people and because they meet their results correctly, it's hard to let them go, but they leave a lot of collateral damage in the process. The best way to have a clear **talent map** is using a graphic where the "x" axis measures people's efficiency, their contribution to the company, their experience or aptitude; the "y" axis measures their attitude, their ways of doing things, their level of accomplishing the values of the company, the way that they behave. Those who mostly meet the values and efficiency are Type A employees; those who have a deficiency in one of the two axes are Type B employees; and those who have a high

deficiency in one of the two axes are Type C employees. Look at the graphic I drew on the board. This matrix has a mistake, which one is it?

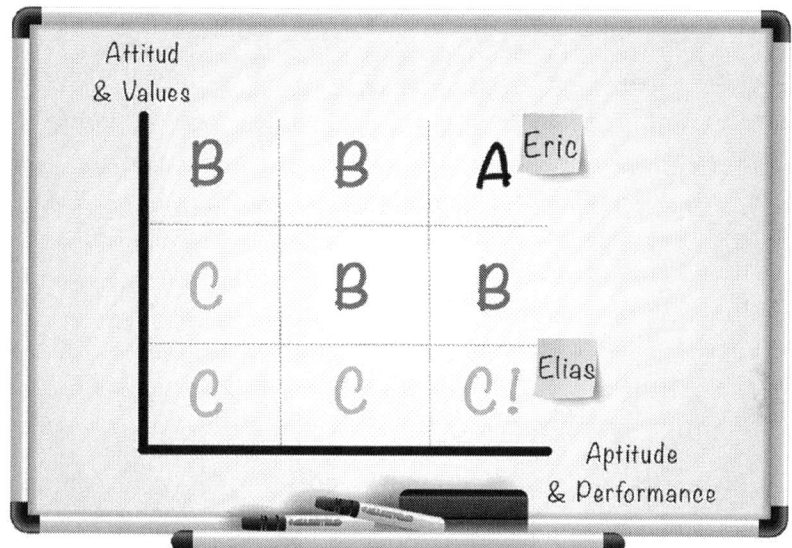

Dan: We'll, I think the "C" at the right. That would be a Type B employee for me.

Rony: That's precisely a "wolf dressed up as a sheep," that's Elias. He's efficient but at any cost.

Dan: I see! Oh, but it would be very difficult not to have him on board. He gets great deals.

Rony: We'll work on that particular situation later. First, I want you to understand the complete model and then you can make your decisions. Let's not get ahead of ourselves. So, what's the mistake in the graphic?

Dan: The "C" down to the left.

Rony: No, that's a genuine "C". It's a constant pain in the neck. It's someone who isn't liked and doesn't provide good results, someone you could fire quickly.

Dan: In that case, the mistake is the letter "C" right on top of the "y" axis, because it is someone who meets the company's values but doesn't provide results. Maybe someone new.

Rony: Correct. Not only could it be someone new, it could also be someone who's going through a hard time personally and because of that his work isn't effective, or someone you changed from their regular position so it's taking him/her time to adjust.

Dan: So, Eric would be in the "A" quadrant?

Rony: Exactly. Now, I want you to evaluate your team with this format and add them to the matrix. Likewise, they should evaluate their colleagues. You should know this is a very powerful tool. It presents reality as it is and if it is not kept confidential we can induce panic at the company. Therefore, the Leadership team shouldn't share the results. It's a tool that will help us make a "diagnosis" or map of the talent you have and make decisions starting from there.

Dan: I get it. Nobody likes to be labeled or to know they might get fired.

Rony: That's right. When can you have the matrix of the company ready so I can meet with you and the leadership team?

Dan: I think in three weeks. Can you meet with us Wednesday three weeks from now?

Rony: Yes, sure. At that meeting, besides analyzing the talent map, I'll explain the employee cycle so we can take action in each one of the steps. This is one of the most crucial steps.

Dan: Perfect. I'll see you in three weeks. I'm excited, I'm already visualizing the Talent map. At least now I have a clearer idea who are the employees I want to keep at the company and those I don't.

Rony: That's the intention. To give you a broad visibility so you can make the right decisions.

On Wednesday morning, before the meeting, I got a text from Dan saying: "Rony, I'm shocked with the result of the Talent map, it seems I have to fire a lot of people. Can we talk?" To which I replied: "I'll arrive 10 minutes before the meeting so we can talk". When I arrived Dan was at his office waiting for me and offered me something to drink.

Dan: Wow, I'm shocked with what this tool showed me and now I'm convinced that over time we hired the wrong people. Our needs pushed us to hire people at any cost and we weren't selective. We have around 25% Type C employees; 70 % Type B and only 5% Type A. We're not going anywhere if we stay like this, and I'm starting to think I'm also in the "B" quadrant. I would've thought I was an "A", but I'm not. I noticed I'm being reactive and distracted. I've had a rage outburst many times in the past few months, and I'm not the best role model. Now I understand what you said about companies who looked like their owners: if I'm a "B" most likely I'd be surrounded by "B's". This was a very painful exercise, seeing the reality of the company and of my leadership.

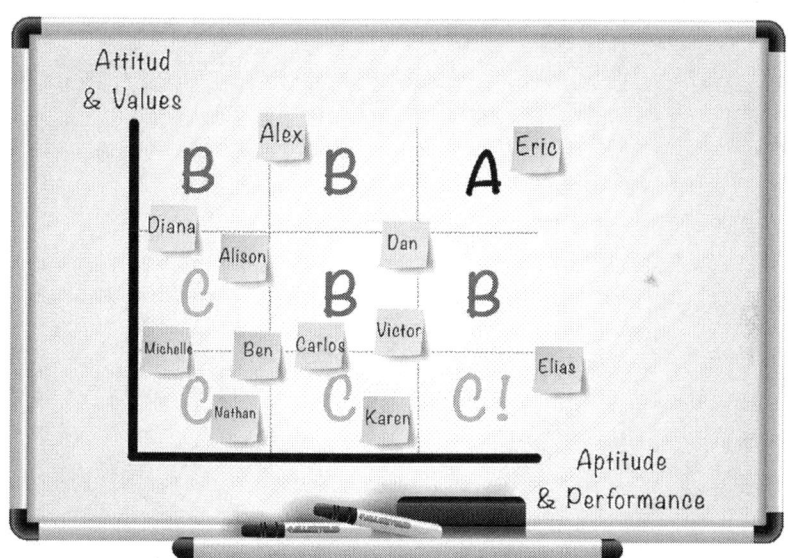

Rony: It's a good thing that you discovered that! I understand the discomfort, but at least for now, you have a very clear picture which will help you make accurate decisions.

Dan: What do you suggest I do?

Rony: My suggestion is: try to find a way to motivate Type A employees; for Type B, besides finding a way to motivate them, we have

to make a plan so they can improve, whether it's their aptitude or their attitude; and for Type C, we should make an exit plan, little by little, even though some of them will leave naturally, because if you show the results publicly and ask for accountability, Type C employees tend to run away They don't like to work in that environment.

Dan: But why let Type C go? We can train them or help them change their behavior or attitude.

Rony: Why make that investment? You already know they're not right for the company. This is not a school, it's a Business. Many owners of companies suffer when they reach this point.

Dan: Of course, I feel emotionally attached to them and to the investment I've made.

Rony: If you have affection for them, you should let them go. The fact that they are in a place where they're not welcome or successful will destroy their self-esteem and opportunities. Remember the example I gave you about Joyce.

Dan: It hurts but I understand. It makes sense. That's why we're in this process, because we have to change things. Once we fire Type C employees we'll have more adequate people, focused on good results, people who are aligned to the culture of the organization and even to our purpose. While having fewer people, our RPE will improve significantly and the organization will be more efficient.

Rony: Now, we have to make decisions along with the team that will lead to important actions so you can attract and keep the best talent. I think we should go to the meeting room and begin.

Rony: Good morning everyone, let's begin our meeting with some good news.

Once all the members of the Leadership team shared their good news we started going deeper on the employee cycle.

Rony: People are the most important element of a company. Besides being the greatest expense on the budget, without a workforce there's no company. Happy employees bring new talent and those who leave angry create a bad reputation. Even when you don't see it, having a

good or bad reputation generates a huge impact on the results of the company, because, where people aren't happy, they're much less efficient and even reach the point of sabotaging the objectives of the company.

Alex: I suppose that's why the Great place to work list exists. It promotes a series of actions and activities we should do to be on it.

Dan: Right now, I don't care if we appear on the Great place to work list. What I do care about is that we implement the philosophy of having happy and productive employees; and eventually, they will bring new candidates to work here.

Rony: Exactly. We're not looking for a certification right now, but we want to apply the principles of GPW. Employees' work life has a defined cycle. We have to consider all the stages an employee goes through, from the attraction, recruiting and selecting, onboarding, development, loyalty/motivation; to the exit, either by firing, retiring or voluntarily leaving.

- **Attraction**. It starts way before there's an opening or someone is hired. Attraction is also known as "employer reputation." It influences **brand recognition** and value. In social media and some web pages like LinkedIn, Glassdor and Apesta.com, employees and former employees post a lot of information about their experience at certain companies. Remember that employees and former employees are those who set the reputation.

- **Selecting/Recruiting**. It's based on hiring the right fit for each position of the organization. Some companies and Experts in human resources display this as being similar to the classic **marketing funnel**. The steps a possible candidate follows in this model are: Exposure, Interest, Active search, Application, assessments and finally, Hiring. The application process is a milestone in the **experience** of candidates. You should ensure this is as simple and likeable as possible. You don't want your customers to go through long and complicated processes of purchase, right? The same applies to people looking for jobs.

> ● **Welcome.** This stage is also known as **onboarding** or **induction.** It helps new employees understand the culture of the company, sets expectations, provides information and the right tools to start working. The more involved and prepared new collaborators feel, the faster they'll bring success to the company. **It's the key to involving the employee in the culture of the company, as it's crucial to ensure they stay at the company.** Around 50% of senior employees leave the company after 18 months of being hired. A right induction process will help employees **understand** what's expected from them. These expectations include the development of intrinsic tasks for the work position and social aspects.

> ● **Development.** Generating learning **expectations** and providing professional opportunities is the best way to cultivate loyalty from those who seek to grow professionally at the company. Statistics show that the lack of career development opportunities is the main reason why employees quit. The main objective is to extend this phase as much as possible to avoid the levels of decreasing motivation, and also that the employee loses productivity and starts considering jumping to the decoupling phase. Career development should be a top priority for employers. Nevertheless, around 70% of employees say they're unsatisfied with the scaling opportunities of the companies where they work.

> ● **Loyalty.** There are many ways for companies to cultivate the loyalty of their employees. Besides, it has been proven that acknowledgment contributes positively to the productivity of collaborators and promotes an open and fluid communication among the employees and the management team. The first step to keep talented employees is quite simple: **listen to them** carefully. It's about understanding what they're going through and finding a way to help them. Keeping talent has a direct impact on the general **development** of organizations. Constantly check the levels of work satisfaction; in the long term you'll be saving time and money. One of the actions that should be applied is a satisfaction survey like ENPS. 40% of employees don't feel appreciated by the companies where they

work. An acknowledgment tool like **StarMeUp** will help you turn corporate values into concrete behaviors. Besides motivating people, you'll have analytics to know in real time what's happening with human talent. You'll be able to acknowledge positive leaders and also anticipate the departure of unsatisfied employees, keeping key people in the company.

> ❶ **Separation.** It's the end of an employee's life cycle. It can happen for different reasons: age, change of job, personal reasons, firing, etc. This is a lesson for the company. This stage is also known as "transition", but in the VUCA environment that we live in, it's important to keep in touch with those professionals who leave the company and turn them into promoters of the brand. When an employee leaves, the rest of the team can feel sad, confused or insecure. Get involved in the transition task and make sure the separation is the least stressful you can make it for everyone.

Alex: That was very instructive! I didn't know the phases we go through as employees. It makes a lot of sense and to be honest, I don't think we are taking care of each one of the employees of the company. I feel we're recruiting people and putting them to work as soon as possible; they learn along the way and suddenly they leave.

Diana: In my former job, I implemented some elements of the employee's life cycle, but here I couldn't do it because I have no time, and also because it wasn't a priority.

Dan: It is now. We should pay attention and implement the right resources to have a good employee cycle. If we build a great team, we can overcome any crisis.

Rony: If by any chance you couldn't manufacture your current product but you have a great team and organizational culture, do you think you could manufacture something else?

Dan: Definitely. It's more difficult to build the right team and have the right talent. Today we sell packages, but if we have a solid team, we can do anything.

Rony: I say we dig deeper on each point of the cycle and define actions that will help us make some progress. **Attraction or reputation.** It's an element that when handled correctly, can attract potential employees. Google has done an amazing job generating an incredible reputation as an employer, up to the point there are even people on waiting lists to work there. In 2018, a company named Blinkist carried out an advertising strategy where they interviewed 1,600 candidates and 73 were hired. Blinkist's acceptance rate was 4.6%, and Harvard's acceptance rate was 5.2%. That way, Blinkist generated the reputation of being an exclusive place to work at, so they generated lots of applicants.

In one of IKEA's stores in Australia they tried to recruit a great number of workers by adding "Career Instructions" to their packages. Every customer that bought one of those packages took a job application without even knowing. This smart initiative not only minimized the costs of advertising, but also attracted IKEA fans. And it worked incredibly! The campaign attracted 4,285 applicants for the job, which turned out into 280 new hirings for their big store. These are creative examples that can help you think of different ways to have a good reputation and attract talent.

Diana: I think we're far away from that; attracting applicants is very hard for us. I've posted job openings on LinkedIn and OCC.com and we never have responses.

Rony: Have you ever heard of https://cofounderslab.com/? Here, you can find candidates and even possible partners. It is a very interesting platform. What else do you think you can do differently?

Alex: I think we can implement a referral program. Like the one we have with our customers. If someone refers us to another customer, we give that person some kind of benefit. We can suggest the same to people who work at the company.

Dan: Excellent idea! Instead of having only one person looking for new talent we can have 70. But we have to be careful that they don't bring the wrong people or people who won't stay long.

Rony: With another client of mine, we implemented a similar process, "referral employees." He established that those candidates who

pass the filter and start working will get 30% of the established bonus, they'll get 40% of the bonus 3 months after their referrals started if they had a good performance; and they'll get the last 30% after 9 months of good performance. So, employees didn't only bring new talent, but also gave follow up and coached them to get their benefits.

Dan: Excellent, I feel we're on the right path. How can we improve the company's reputation so we can be on the radar of possible employees?

Victor: We could build houses for people in need with wasted materials; that way, our employees will feel they're contributing something to society and the people we helped will talk about us.

Carlos: We could even publish our work in college newspapers so that students will know our company and our labor.

Rony: **Recruiting and selecting.** Companies spend a lot of time on this process because if you post a position online, people apply without reading the instructions, which makes companies select and minimize the candidates that will go through to the next stage of the interview. A strategy that has been successful to sort candidates is to hide instructions in the post. For example, they write Pennsylvania69 somewhere and further on it says: "If you reached this point and found the key (a city and a number) which you will use as the email subject, please send your CV on PDF along with a picture of you as a kid". Like that, the HR department only checks the emails with the subject "Pennsylvania69" that have a PDF and a picture of a kid attached. This way, they eliminate about 80% of applicants who send their applications to every company and position they find. For the interviews it's not only important to evaluate the technical abilities (aptitudes) of the candidates, but also that their attitude is appropriate for the culture of the company. A great example of this was Heineken's "behavioral interviews". These are interviews you can't prepare for, because they measure how you react to certain situations. For example, if you had to help firefighters during an emergency or if the interviewer takes you by the hand and leads you towards where the interview is taking place. After interviewing all candidates, Heineken published in-house the

three best applicants so the marketing team could pick the right one. The most voted candidate was invited to a match of the Champions League at the Juventus stadium, which was sponsored by Heineken, and they projected a video on the big screens of the stadium showing who was officially picked for the job. In addition, they edited and published the video with the title "Heineken candidate" to generate reputation for the company. The video reached 816,000 viewers in three days.

Rony: Another strategy is asking candidates to do some kind of homework before the interview, such as writing a letter directed to the community leader where they can suggest ideas to improve things. If the candidate arrives without the letter, there's no need to interview that person. If the candidate arrives with the letter, you can read it and understand the way that person thinks about other people and his disposition to improve things.

Diana: I think the first two ideas are very hard to apply in our company, but we could definitely ask them for the letter.

Dan: I would love it if people could read a book before the interview and bring a paper with what they learned. It could be book FISH, by Stephen C. Lundin

Rony: **Welcome and onboarding.** The experience of the first day of work generates attachment and love towards the company. The day I started working at Nestlé Switzerland, someone was waiting for me outside the building, walked me to my desk, which had my badge, my business cards, a pack of pens which are very appreciated in that environment, and they organized lunch with my boss and a couple of colleagues. They made me feel very special.

Victor: I've seen people posting pictures of their desks on Instagram on their first day of work. They have a shirt with the company's logo and their names on it, a backpack, a notebook and some candies.

Dan: A friend of mine sends a bouquet of flowers to the wives of his new employees with a note that says: "Welcome to the UXF family. Thank you for sharing your husband's talent with us".

Alex: And if they're women?

Dan: They send a bottle of wine to the husbands which they can share with their wives while talking about their first day.

Diana: We definitely need to put into practice some of these ideas, and new employees have to be trained properly. We should show them the facilities, tell them the story and philosophy of the company, share the organization chart with them and train them according to the area where they're working. We can't assume they know the machinery we work with.

Rony: **Development.** As Michael Dell, the founder of Dell computers said, "hire smart and keep them smart". According to the company "Statistica", in 2019 small companies trained their employees for approximately 49 hours. At Statistica, they consider those who have 100 to 999 employees as small companies. (https://www.statista.com/statistics/795813/hours-of-training-per-employee-by-company-size-us/)

Diana: We have around 20 hours of training per year.

Dan: We should definitely improve our training and the time we invest in employees. I think we should have a training program at the company for new employees. We can't keep hiring people and put them to work right away. We should train them at least for a week, teach them about the areas of the company and introduce them to their colleagues. It would be great that the training program goes through every area of the company following the right order from beginning to end or from planning to delivering.

Rony: We have to make sure that the people who work at the company have both personal and professional training. That includes machinery training, administration, finances and any other element that lets your staff become a better talent.

Victor: I fear that we train people and the competition steals them. I don't want us to become another company's university.

Dan: So, would you rather have mediocre employees or with less knowledge?

Victor: Of course not, but one of the problems we have is that people leave.

Alex: So we have to find a way to prevent people from wanting to leave the company, but we definitely have to provide complete training. At my former job, I began working with a lot of enthusiasm and knowledge. At the beginning, I felt I was learning and making a lot of progress, but after two years of not getting any training, I was just working to fulfill my responsibilities; I felt stuck.

Rony: And what happens when people start to feel stuck and frustrated?

Diana: They look for other options or start doing things against the culture of the company, like sabotage and gossip.

Victor: I get the point. I think it is better if we invest in staff development and training, but we have to make plans to ensure people stay. I'm tired of staff turnover. Each time someone leaves or we hire someone new, we need to start over and the company's productivity drops.

Rony: That's precisely the next point: **Loyalty.** How can we make employees feel at home, proud of their workplace and not wanting to leave? For starters, we have already talked about some elements that can help, like training and the right admission process. Other elements that could help are: acknowledgement, a leader who listens to them, the possibility of contributing to the company, schedule flexibility, benefits like medical insurance, competitive salary, labor autonomy. I really like the discovery Daniel Pink made from his research and which he reflected on in his book: Drive; *The surprising truth about what motivates us.* In a very simple way he says we shall fulfill MAPs: Mastery, Autonomy, Purpose and salary. If we fulfill those four elements we can motivate employees wonderfully. Let's look through each element starting with the most obvious one, salary. Each employee of the company should have a competitive salary related to his functions. If people have a good salary, they won't be thinking about other ways to bring money home; now's the right moment to say: "If you pay peanuts you get monkeys."

Rony: *Mastery,* as the name says, is about being able to master the tasks that were assigned to us. If we want someone from the maintenance team to have excellent knowledge about his area to the

point of becoming a master it can lead to *Autonomy*, which is the desire of directing oneself, making defining decisions and being in charge of results, which leads to accountability. And last but not least, *Purpose*, it's giving our tasks and activities a worthy purpose, people who contribute to everything.

Dan: I have to say that for a while I wanted to pay salaries as low as possible, until I understood the impact that not having the right people at the company had. At the beginning, making the investment was hard, but little by little we got so we could hire the right people and had better results.

Diana: Here we do not make positive acknowledgements. We know exactly how to tell people off when they do something wrong, but we're not good at acknowledging good actions or contributions from employees. I think we should implement a monthly meeting where we can acknowledge people who achieve extraordinary results. I've seen acknowledgment programs from other companies which create a sense of motivation and love towards the company. We can give pins as if they were soldiers who accomplished an important mission; for sure they would wear it proudly and share their acknowledgment with their families.

Dan: I love the idea. At that meeting we should also present the results of the company. It's time for everyone to know the status and direction of the company.

Rony: We can also use that meeting to celebrate people's birthdays. So, in that meeting you can present the results of the last month, the objectives and priorities of the next month, acknowledge employees and celebrate their birthdays.

Carlos: Besides having people informed and motivated, we are all going to be on the same page, knowing exactly where we came from and where we are going.

Rony: Another tool that improves employee's loyalty and development is monthly feedback meetings or performance reviews, where you can review their results, attitudes, training, etc. It's the right time to let them know if they're performing correctly.

Alex: So if someone makes a mistake, we have to wait for that monthly evaluation meeting to tell them?

Rony: No, not at all. If someone makes a mistake they have to know ASAP, and if they do something good you should also acknowledge them ASAP. The meeting of performance review should be formal. You have to give feedback privately and make a work plan together so that employees can be better.

Victor: I like that model. That way I'll have enough information at the end of the month to deal with each person or situation at the meeting.

Dan: In my case, as CEO, should I also be giving feedback once a month?

Rony: Yes, but in your case, it should be a weekly reunion with each director of the company, so you can help them make progress and they can keep you posted with the details of what's happening in their departments. These are practical sessions where you can coach them.

Dan: So by coaching, do you mean ask them a bunch of questions and not give them the answer?

Rony: Exactly. the objective of those meetings is to lead them and teach them how to make decisions based on your way of thinking. It's about teaching them to solve problems and help them see the complete picture of the company from your own perspective, so you won't have to solve every problem.

Dan: Once a week? It sounds a lot, and besides, I don't know how to do it.

Rony: If today you count how much time you spend meeting every day with each one of the directors it would for sure add up to more than 60 minutes. The difference here is that you'll know you have a designated time every week to address certain things, so it will decrease the number of interruptions you have every week, and everyone, including you, is going to be prepared for that meeting. About your question of how to do it, I suggest you use the **GROW** coaching model: Goal, Reality, Options or Obstacles and Way forward.

The conversation with the team went on and more ideas came up. The group's enthusiasm rose as they shared their ideas and solutions.

Rony: **Separation** is something we have to consider. Employees will eventually leave the company. Nobody here, not even you Dan, will be here forever, so we have to anticipate how to handle that issue correctly. There are three types of separation: voluntary, firing or retirement.

Alex: Death is also separation.

People laughed nervously.

Diana: We should have a protocol to know how to address each situation, a series of steps we can use to respond systematically. For example, if a colleague dies we have to call the insurance company, send flowers to the family, and post it in the company's board of ceremony information.

Victor: I would be happy knowing this company cares about me, even if I'm not here.

Rony: In any scenario the separation should be honorable. We have to treat people well when they leave. Remember, they will be your voice out there and will generate a big part of the company's reputation. Leaving voluntarily could be because people are searching for new opportunities, such as a job in another company or becoming an entrepreneur. Firing someone is when the company decides that a person should go. It generally happens because of bad development or aptitude, or also a bad attitude towards the values of the organization. Remember the Talent Map you made, where you mapped people according to their attitude vs aptitude. Retirement is the moment when people fulfill a cycle either for their age or for the number of years working. They should get compensation according to the law. Some companies decide to support the people who leave the company with a process named "outplacement," which consists of assisting or coaching former employees so they can find work at another company or adjust to their new life. Can you imagine what happens with someone who's worked for 35 years at the same company, woke up every day at the same time and got ready to leave at 7 a.m.?

Dan: Even if they're not working any more they're ready to leave at 7 a.m. without even knowing where to go. The father of one of my friends was retired and didn't know what to do with his life, so he kept following the same routine but without having anything to do. Fortunately, he found a way to keep busy, because I've heard of some people who have nothing to do and die a couple years after they retire.

Rony: So, which other actions should we implement here?

Diana: We have to interview each person who leaves. These are called "exit interviews."

Carlos: This is going to sound crazy, but what if we throw a little goodbye party for those who leave?

Dan: What for? We should throw a welcome party instead for new employees.

Rony: Both parties are excellent ideas. you can do the same party for both purposes: those who are new you can welcome, and to those who leave you can say thank you.

Victor: Why throw a party to someone who leaves the company for bad development?

Dan: To celebrate they are finally leaving.

Everyone laughed and the conversation kept going for a while, finding new ideas and solutions that the team placed in the action plan.

Conclusions:

- Having the right people or "collaboration community" is the key to taking the organization to the next stage. You should map the talent and make specific plans according to the result.
- The path traveled hasn't been easy, but it has given you the visibility and clarity to make difficult decisions as to which products, customers and employees you should keep working with. Now, you have to work on another pillar of the company, suppliers.

13 SUPPLIERS THAT REALLY SUPPORT GROWTH.

> ❱ If the input in the system is bullshit, don't expect something different in the output.
>
> ❱ Having a base of reliable suppliers will help make better decisions and have better control over the variables that could have a direct impact on the possibility of offering the services and products we commit to.

Rony: The Yak Yak telemarketing group from Pakistan outsourced their telephonic telemarketing program to The Hello Telemarketing Agency, whose headquarters were in Cleveland. The Yak Yak agency, which was the third largest in the country, decided it would be more productive to have American telephonic representatives and agents than Pakistanis. They made this decision because according to market research, it was demonstrated that when they received calls at the Pakistan call center, operators spent a lot of time trying to explain the same thing over and over because the customers didn't understand what they said. The research that lasted six months concluded that customers kept repeating the phrase: "Can you repeat that again? I'm sorry, I don't understand you" at least 87,000 times a day, which is a lot considering they received 22,000 calls per day, and which represents an average of 3.95 times per call.

Dan: Really? It's very ironic that a call center from Pakistan hired a service from the USA.

Rony: The example isn't real its just a joke, but it portrays correctly the importance of hiring the right supplier for your operation.

Dan: Of course, if customers don't understand the operator of the call center, they will have a bad experience and the company will have a bad reputation. According to the email you sent me about this Supplier Categorization meeting, I suppose we're going to work with a similar process as we did with employees, customers and products, to figure out which suppliers we should keep working with.

Rony: That's right. We should check the company 360 degrees to ensure every part counts and has the best resources.

Dan: After everything that we've done and the decisions we've made along the process, I no longer have fear of making the analysis and decisions according to suppliers.

Rony: It's good knowing you already have confidence and security.

Dan: The truth is that this process has helped me trust myself and the leadership team. The decisions we make now are more rational and objective. We already have the right methodology and framework.

Rony: Well, let's start with the designated task for today. Suppliers are your commercial partners. Their success depends on yours and vice versa. Do you have reliable and stable suppliers that ensure the success of the company?

Dan: Mostly I do, but there are some suppliers whose chaos impacts on the organization, so I have to get more raw material due to the uncertainty because I don't know if they will still be making it. This translates into higher costs, lower profit, and space in the warehouse that could be used for other products.

Rony: In case one of the suppliers fades or declares bankruptcy, do you have someone to replace them?

Dan: Actually, no. I haven't thought about that situation even when it has happened before, and when it does, we just go on an emergency search of who can be the replacement.

Rony: As you have your virtual bench of employees in case someone leaves and a pipeline of prospects to be converted into clients, you should also have a backup of suppliers that ensures the continuity of the company. Remember we have to shield the company and ensure

continuity. Suppliers are another pillar that will help the company succeed.

Dan: For the polyethylene raw material, which is the main material of our company, we have several reliable suppliers, because there's a lot of supply on the market and also because it is the key to my daily operation. Before, it was a situation that kept me up at night because we only had one reliable supplier, and because he knew he was the only one, he tended to be abusive, and from time to time, he changed prices and conditions and drove me crazy, so I decided to search for an alternative supplier.

Rony: It sounds like the situation of Victor, that you felt trapped with him because you had no other option.

Dan: Exactly, I was trapped.

Rony: You have to be able to trust that they will deliver in a timely manner and also that the company is stable enough to last so you can make long term commitments. That's the key. This is commonly known as Suppliers Management. According to the norm ISO 9001 which establishes that: "The organization should evaluate and select suppliers based on its capacity to supply products according to the requirements of the organization." A series of criteria should be established for selecting, evaluating and re-evaluating suppliers. In order to have a real advantage in the supply chain, it is required to have more efficient logistic processes. Their strategy has to be aligned with the strategy and the general objectives of the company; therefore, the supply chain goals have to be set according to a series of criteria like the cost, quality, availability, delivery deadlines, service and payment methods. Sometimes, these criteria can make the process of selecting suppliers really hard, because it is eminently subjective and significant differences can be produced in the classification of the same supplier, according to the person who makes the evaluation.

Dan: But how can I eliminate subjectivity from the process of selecting suppliers with concrete tools?

Rony: That's precisely something we're going to work on. Which is the most important criterion you have when you evaluate suppliers?

Dan: I don't have one in particular, but definitely, quality, price, on-time deliveries, credit line and others.

Rony: Some years ago I entered a drycleaner where they had a sign: "We can offer 3 different services: Quality, Price and Speed. You can pick 2 of them". The quality and price won't be fast. The speed and quality won't be cheap. The speed and cheap won't be good quality.

Dan: Very good and illustrative example.

Rony: Picking the right suppliers is a multi-criteria decision and it has a strategic impact. You should identify the most important characteristics of your company knowing they won't meet all your expectations. The supplier selection has been studied and developed by many researchers and scholars. Models and forms of supplier management have existed since 1966. Dickson was the first person who searched for important criteria to select suppliers. He identified and analyzed the importance of 23 criteria and concluded that **quality** was the most important, followed by **on time** deliveries and a good history of **development** of the organization. In the 80's businessmen

in the US considered four basic competitive priorities: **cost, flexibility, quality and delivery.** In the early 90s, a literature review published by Weber, Current and Bentom (1991), based on the analysis of 74 scientific articles, established that the most important priorities were **quality** and **delivery accuracy.** Back then, people started to talk about two new competitive priorities: **service** and **innovation.** In the late 90's and earlier in this century, a new priority was found: **social and environmental responsibility.** Chen and Li (2005) did research where they analyzed different proposals from different authors regarding the importance each one of the criteria had in the selection process. The result of that investigation concluded that **quality** was the number one. Goffin and Lemke (2006) highlighted that having good relationships with suppliers reduced costs for the manufacturers, improved quality and the development of new products. Huang and Keskar (2007) said that the fundamental element to ensure the success of supplier selection was to carefully determine criteria that met the strategy and the goals of the company. They also highlighted the importance of continually reviewing and updating criteria and analyzing the level of agreement with the conditions of the market and the competition. I think the key is not only on one criterion but in the combination of several elements: you have to evaluate many things that can give you the final number to categorize your suppliers, and as a result, you'll get **RELIABILITY,** which is the combination of several evaluated elements that provide the level of reliability. There's no universal formula for categorizing suppliers because it depends on the industry, the culture of the country and many other elements.

Dan: I agree, I can't only consider price or quality as the unique factors to pick my suppliers. In fact, not so long ago I had a prospect that was looking for a new package supplier for his new product. Turns out we both belong to a similar association and have friends in common. Even though my product is a little more expensive and my delivery logistics take a little longer, this prospect decided to work with us because, in his own words, "One has to grow close to your network, because if someone wins, we all win." I wish there were more people who

think like him. We would live in a world where people's mindset would be abundance and collaboration, instead of scarcity and selfishness.

Rony: There are 7 main steps you have to know about supplier management:

- Supplier search
- Selection
- Keep in touch with backups
- Due diligence
- Verify operations
- Supplier development
- Budgeting

Rony: Let's talk about **supplier search.** You should understand your problem and think about someone who can fix it. Having that information will make your search easier. Can you imagine someone who was looking for fruit in the electronics department?

Dan: No, that would be a waste of time.

Rony: Well, this happens in many companies: They have an urgent need so they pick the first supplier they find who can solve their problem without understanding their needs, problems or company expectations. Here's where Alex, the director of Finances and Administration can help. The procurement department is one of his duties, so the buyer has to follow the protocols established by the company to search for new suppliers and deal with those who already work with you. This person has to get the request to search for new suppliers, preferably in writing, with a very clear explanation of the needs of the internal customer.

Dan: That way, his search could be more effective. I've always wanted to institutionalize "three price quotations" for one need so we can make better decisions and have alternatives.

Rony: You're walking down the right path. That exercise is fundamental to promote healthy competition among suppliers and transparency in the organization.

Dan: A few years ago, the guy who was our procurement manager always brought just one price quotation. Then we discovered the numbers were inflated and the supplier was paying a commission to our buyer, which led to a conflict of interests. I was paying him to take care of our interests, not his. When we discovered this, I fired both the buyer and the supplier because they abused my trust and did things the wrong way. Since then, I wanted to implement something that could prevent this situation from happening, apart from the fact that I review many of the purchases made and give the final authorization.

Rony: How much time do you spend reviewing purchases? What do you overlook?

Dan: A lot of time. It's one of the many tasks I shouldn't be doing, but I do it because of lack of trust and a work methodology. What do I overlook? Well, to be honest I overlook many valuable things like not being with customers, reviewing plans of development, training and others.

Rony: Even though we are moving a few steps forward, you're right. Let's go back to the supplier search. So, a person gets the internal request with the details of the needs, restrictions, times and other elements. That way, the buyer can start looking for suppliers. There are many ways to do it, LinkedIn, Google, Chambers of Commerce, recommendations. Nowadays, people always search for everything in Google, but they don't go beyond. You would be surprised by the recommendations you can get from the people you know like business owners or buyers. You just have to call the procurement areas of other companies who aren't your competitors and work with similar suppliers.

Dan: I had never thought the buyer of another company could refer me to one of their suppliers.

Rony: For sure! If they have a mindset of "Abundance" they will. At the end of the day, it's a win-win situation because it's good for him that his supplier is more stable and has more customers.

Dan: But most people think their success depends on others' failure.

Rony: Yes, but little by little you'll find people that have this collaborative mindset. By the way, it's normal if there are tasks that

are required from someone specialized in something you can't handle, like designing a logo, writing a script or things like that. There's an extraordinary platform where you can hire specific services from well prepared people for a lot less than hiring someone full time. The name of the platform is Fiverr. There you can find freelance services ideal for your company. There's also another webpage named Topcoder, with professional people who offer services like programming web pages, apps, data and science.

Rony: **Selection.**

Dan: To select suppliers we should do things differently than we do today. We should have a list of steps to follow to select suppliers; we should have samples and laboratory tests.

Rony: Besides, you should trust that it's an established company, which has prices and times consistent with you. The most practical way of doing this is to build an evaluation matrix where you should place suppliers, different criteria to evaluate and give each criteria a different weight; that way, the process will be objective.

Dan: But there are also subjective things we have to consider, like for example if there's an important relationship, if I like them or not, if I trust them or not. These elements can't be measured with numbers.

Rony: Of course they can. Everything can be measured with numbers. For example, from 0 to 10, how much do you trust your cleaning and maintenance supplier?

Dan: I see. These qualitative attributes can turn into quantitative. This matrix will definitely help us make the supplier selection process more objective, because there can be many factors involved when making the decision. It can become overwhelming to the point where sometimes we can make decisions based on only one or two elements. But on the supplier selection matrix we will place all the attributes we want to evaluate and as a result, it will give us a number.

Rony: That precise number is the one I mentioned before, RELIABILITY. The balance of all the attributes will clarify which supplier is more reliable than the other. This will help you make more transparent, objective, and beneficial decisions for the company.

Rony: **Keep in touch with backups.**

Dan: I suppose that as we have the Virtual bench of employees and the pipeline of customers and prospects, we should also have a list of suppliers.

Rony: Wow, you are a few steps ahead of me, I'm glad. That list is called "supplier backup." It's very important to have it updated and complete so you can use it not only if any of your suppliers fails you, but also because you have no guarantee that your buyer will stay at the company. Remember we have to protect the company at any cost and having this list will help you take quick action in case of an emergency.

Rony: **Due diligence.** Unfortunately, nowadays there are many frauds or illicit operations. You don't want to be involved with a supplier whose operation is at risk because they are not paying taxes, not able to legally create invoices, have a significant amount of lawsuits, or even worse, have exploitative child labor.

Dan: I definitely don't want to be involved with anything like that.

Rony: When was the last time you reviewed the documentation of your suppliers or that someone went to their facilities to do a field auditing?

Dan: The last time? We have never done that. Each time we hire a new supplier they come to our facilities.

Rony: You can do this process yourself or hire a law firm or consultancy to do it for you, but it's something very important you should do.

Dan: But that implies adding another step to the process We can become bureaucratic.

Rony: I know it means adding another step to the process, but it will help you know your suppliers better. I've heard horror stories where people start working with a supplier whose operation is very critical for the success of the company, and a few months later, they disappear. For example, in Mexico there's a big problem in the food industry for sugar supply because there are some scoundrels that create ghost

companies with very professional web pages that offer sugar containers at a very good price, so it makes them attractive. Turns out that many candy factories were attracted to their price because sugar is their main product, and they were persuaded by the good image that these scoundrels had online and started buying from them. At first, it was one container, and then, more and more. When they reach a good level of trust, these scoundrels start to change payment conditions asking for an advanced payment of some of the shipments of the month, thanks to the trust they generated with past deliveries, the factory agrees. The next month, they ask for an advance payment of the entire shipment of the month; the factory naturally agrees and that is when they disappear. The web page is deleted, nobody knows where the facilities are, their documentation was false; anyway, they end up stealing large amounts of money.

Dan: I understand, and all of this can be avoided by reviewing their documentation and facilities?

Rony: Not entirely, but it reduces the risk. Unfortunately, there are lots of frauds and illicit operations like using children for the labor force, inhumane working conditions and more.

Dan: As I mentioned before, I don't want to be part of any of that. We'll start implementing the due diligence.

Rony: **Supplier development.**

Dan: About that, what do you mean by developing suppliers?

Rony: With time, the company grows and blossoms, demanding more attention, precision, resources, credit lines. In most cases, suppliers, as well as employees, don't grow at the same speed as the company, which might be a risk for long term plans.

Dan: It makes sense. If we outgrow my suppliers they can't keep providing the service that I need, so I have to search for new suppliers that meet my needs. But my business is not developing suppliers.

Rony: That's right, but it's in your interest that they make progress and grow.

Dan: And what do I need to do to develop them?

Rony: You have to identify key suppliers for the company, whether for the product or service they offer. And those who you think are worthy, you'll develop. This can happen in many ways: training, on-time payment, simplified administrative process, among other things.

Dan: Training? Now I think you're going crazy... How am I going to train them?

Rony: A couple of weeks ago you hired a consultant to give Personal Finances Training. You filled the main conference room with all your employees but still had some seats available. If you would have invited some of your suppliers to take the same training, it would have helped them improve their personal and organizational development.

Dan: That's an excellent idea! And it wouldn't have been an expense. I get the idea. I didn't think of it that way. To be honest, suppliers aren't on my radar, but now I know I have to make sure they are in the right place so my company can keep improving. You mentioned on-time payment. We always do what we need to do to pay on time. Still, I would like to know why that is so important for this issue?

Rony: Not paying your suppliers on time not only gives you a bad reputation with the people who can refer you to new customers and new employees, but you also take the risk that, for your lack of payment, they get distracted with things that aren't important like providing the right service or product to you. Not paying on time damages the relationship and profitability of their company.

Dan: I know many CEOs that take advantage of the payment time they give to their suppliers so they can have a stable company with cash flow.

Rony: I think that's a very bad strategy because they're shooting themselves in the foot. Suppliers are an essential part of your company, they are an extra gear, and if the result isn't good, guess who's going to be damaged.

Dan: Us, and then our customers.

Rony: I understand there can be exceptions, unfortunate situations where you won't be able to pay. When something like that happens, the best thing to do is to be honest with your suppliers, the same way you would want your clients to treat you.

Dan: I have to apply the golden rule: treat others as you would like to be treated.

Rony: I couldn't have said it better.

Rony: **Budgeting.** Tell me about your budgets. Do you have clear budgets that can lead the decisions of the company?

Dan: Having the right budget has been difficult for me the last few years. The truth is, the expenses of the company are a little out of control; I'm the first to blame because I use the company's credit card without checking our line of credit.

Rony: One of the most common mistakes entrepreneurs make, even those who have been operating for several years, is not **developing budgets.** The reason is the lack of knowledge and attention or simply believing that "selling a lot" would be enough. Financial forecasts are a very important tool to have a healthy and sustainable administration. Having a budget forces you to prepare a financial overview over the next couple of months, to have a better understanding of the given results and to **make the best decisions.** Establishing milestones, revenue, costs and profits, are some of the main virtues of any successful entrepreneur.

Dan: I really understand the theory and how important it is to have a budget, but it just hasn't been my priority.

Rony: Having a well-made budget helps measure the growing capacity of the company. It shows you how to distribute your resources and helps you find out if the capital you have or are raising is enough.

Dan: I think I haven't moved forward with budgets because I feel it's a complicated matter that will make the company bureaucratic.

Rony: A budget can be as complicated or as easy as you decide, according to the stage of development the company is at. Whether you write it on a piece of paper or use an Excel format, the important characteristics that it has to include are:

- Sales and revenue projection
- Projection of the total costs to reach the level of sales projected.
  - Fixed cost and variable cost should include:
    - Sales or manufacture of the product and/or service
    - Merchandising
    - Delivery
    - Sales and marketing
    - Administration and operation
- Profits and losses projection (as a result of the two previous numbers)
- Total Cumulative profits and losses projected through time (during a certain period of time)

Dan: I do indeed commit to do an Excel format along with Alex so we can handle the budget.

Rony: Why do it along with Alex? Isn't it his responsibility? Remember the power of delegating.

Dan: Right, so I'll ask him to do it and show it to me, though he'll probably need my perspective.

Rony: By the way, are you receiving salary or are you milking the profits of the company?

Dan: Ha ha. I have a very basic salary so if I need more money, I withdraw it.

Rony: That's something you shouldn't do because it creates uncertainty and is unpredictable. Besides, you don't necessarily have to cash out every month.

Dan: So what do you suggest?

Rony: That you have a salary according to your position. It has to be competitive. If you need more cash you can withdraw it as company profits.

Dan: And what difference does it make? What are the benefits?

Rony: The difference is that you'll have a fixed salary, a budgeted cost of the company, and it provides stability and certainty for both

the company and your family. About the benefits, the most important one is that the company will be used to pay a salary for your position and one day, when you want to hire a CEO to replace you, the salary won't be an obstacle because the company will be used to having it in the budget. Let me tell you the story of another customer of mine. He owns 17 restaurants in Mexico City. He had no assigned salary, so he used his restaurants as ATMs, which caused a series of administrative problems, above all, between the managers of the restaurants and the general manager of the company, who was demanding that they not give money to the owner so he had to go to the headquarters. The managers answered: "Are you really asking me to say no to the boss?"

Dan: It makes sense. To have a fixed salary will be a challenge. I think I'll start with a low salary and then, over time, I'll increase it.

Rony: That's so much better than what you do today.

Conclusions:

- ❯ Suppliers are a key part of the manufacturing chain and the results of the company. You have to work with the most reliable suppliers that ensure that you can provide the best service and product to your customers.

- ❯ Organizational change and growth are more bearable when working with the right people and having support, or in the right environment.

 ENVIRONMENT THAT PROMOTES GROWTH.

> ❱ Being the leader of an organization is a very lonely position.
>
> ❱ Anyone can be successful if they work in the right environment which promotes their success. This includes Mastermind groups, consultants, using the best practices in the industry, having strategic alliances, advisory boards, and possible groups of investors.

I arrived at Dan's office for his coaching session and surprisingly, it was organized. For the first time since we've met, he didn't have papers all over the place, post its on every wall; finally, there was order and he seemed relaxed.

Dan: Good morning, I'm glad you're here! Many things have changed these past few weeks. People left, some we had to ask to leave. You can feel a kinder, results-oriented and less dramatic environment now. Some of our customers, particularly those who are in the "Top 10", have started to notice positive changes, and said they're happy with these changes.

Rony: That's very good to know! The idea was to grow the company in an organized way, make it profitable, and that people are happy. I noticed your office is very organized too.

Dan: Yes, I realized that not only the company was disorganized but also my office, my mind and my house. So, I remembered once you said, "A company is the reflection of its leader," so I got to thinking

about the type of company that I want to have and reflect it. This is what I want, an organized and efficient company. I have to be a role model, and what better way to reflect organization than through my office?

Rony: Well congratulations, that was a very mature decision. How was the exit of "C employees"?

Dan: As you said and to my surprise, some decided to leave on their own because they didn't want to be measured, and with others we had to make the decision ourselves. The geat surprise was that "A employees" came to congratulate me for the decision I made of letting people go, especially Elias, who was generating a very toxic work environment. Do you remember the wolf dressed as a sheep? They even told me it took me long enough to realize he wasn't the right fit for the company.

Rony: Wow, that's music to my ears. Well, now's the time to start working on the environment, even though you already taken a few steps forward.

Dan: Environment?

Rony: Yes, the environment is the support "tool" that will help you improve constantly. I used to think there were successful and unsuccessful people. I thought the differences between them were the attitudes, abilities and a lot of personal development. The truth is there aren't successful and unsuccessful people; anyone can be successful if they are surrounded by the right environment. A soldier can be powerful, brave and organized in a military environment, but if he changes his environment, that same person can have problems reaching the basic levels of social environment. A Google employee can create an app that reaches 10 million users, but if you take that person out of Google he can have problems starting a new business that reaches 10,000 people.

Dan: Once I heard that your incomes are the average of the 10 people you spend the most time with.

Rony: According to Jim Rohn it's five people: "You're the average of the five people you spend the most time with". Only five people around you determine your success!

Dan: I think I have to make a selection of the people surrounding me. There are a couple of people I want to take out of my circle. They are toxic and instead of helping me grow they tear me down.

Right there I stood up and wrote this formula on the flip chart: +x>-/

Rony: Maybe it's time for you to apply the +x>-/ formula. It means: **"it's better to add and multiply than to subtract and divide".** Think of it as a scale; one side is for those who add value and energy to your life, and the other side is for those who subtract value or energy from your life. That's an easy way to evaluate the people around you. For example, have trustworthy consultants, strategic alliances, Mastermind groups, possible investors and advisory boards.

Dan: If we continue improving like this, I think we're on our way to achieving that. We are much better organized. Consultants, well, we have you and we're about to hire another person who can help us improve the maintenance plan of the machinery, as that has been a problem. I would like to know more about the other aspects. I'm not familiar with them.

Rony: Of course, that's the idea, not only will I tell you about them, you will make decisions to complement the company with the people you need. Let's start with possible **investors or lenders.** Thinking a little catastrophic, in case the company has a complicated economic problem, is there someone you can ask for money ?

Dan: Well, as they say, FFF: friends, family and fools. But I don't know how far I can go with them, because they were the financial sources at the beginning. I already repaid all of them, but I wouldn't feel comfortable having them as investors again. I would rather keep friends and family apart from the company.

Rony: So in case you need a group of investors or people who lend you money, is there someone you can ask for money?

Dan: Not really. No one comes to my mind right now, but I'll make a list of people that could help me in case I need money for the company. Now tell me about the advisory board.

Rony: The **advisory board** is a monthly or quarterly meeting where you expose the results of the company and the strategic plan. The attendees are businessmen and people you trust who want to support you with the development and success of the company. You show them the results the company had in that period of time. You tell them the problems you have and they give you ideas, solutions, and questions that will help you make better decisions. They do it because they want what's best for the company, and as they don't belong to the same industry, they give you a very different perspective. Imagine the advisory board of someone who develops software is constituted by the owner of a restaurant and the owner of a clothing factory. You'll be surprised how the experiences of other industries can contribute to your company. Besides, the cherry on top of the cake or the best part is that you'll have a team who will hold you accountable.

Dan: Wait, what? Hold me accountable? Now you want me to have people pressuring me?

Rony: No, not pressuring you, but it's a fact that human beings are experts at self-deception and procrastinating. We tend to do things at the last minute. If we don't have someone who holds us accountable, we deceive ourselves. Remember the lesson of accountability, it's the only system that allows people to achieve high results. The advisors won't care whether you meet your commitments or not, they're going to be the tool that'll make you feel the need to meet them, as employees with you. You are going to be the one who cares about presenting your results to the board. Do you remember the dentist phenomenon?

Dan: Yes, the practice of people washing their teeth before going to their dental appointment, which doesn't make any sense if they have been doing it right all along. It means people make an extra effort to meet their desired results. I get the idea. I just think I have to test it and see if it works for me. I have mixed feelings; on one hand, I want to go to those meetings to listen to different perspectives, but on the other, I wouldn't like to feel like an employee.

Rony: Don't worry, you won't feel like an employee. We'll all be there to support you. It will be a meeting to give you different perspectives

DONT LET THE TAIL WAG THE DOG

and push you to be better. Besides, it's a huge step so the company and you can be ready for it, when you decide it's time for another CEO to replace you, and when that happens, the new CEO will be presenting his plans to the advisory board, and he will be accountable for the operation of the company; and you'll be part of the board.

Dan: Now I like the idea. But it will take some time for another CEO to replace me.

Rony: While that happens, you can make a habit of attending these meetings. It will be good for you and prepare you for the next level. Besides, the attendees can present other business to you. Now let's talk about **Mastermind.** This term was coined by Napoleon Hill in his book *Think and grow rich,* where he explains the power and potential of belonging to a group of people with aligned purposes. Imagine that you gather with a group of six to 10 businessmen once a month, each of them from a different industry, for the purpose of helping each other improve and achieve better results. It's not a networking meeting where you'll seek new customers or referrals, it's another type of group.

Dan: Are you serious? Businessmen gathered without doing business with each other? What do they do then?

Rony: We gather every month to share the results of the commitments we made at the last meeting. We have training and a space to talk about problems that we have, either personal or work-related.

Dan: And why would I share my personal problems with a group of strangers?

Rony: The people in the group will stop being strangers to you very fast. It will become a support group and creative thinking space. You'll find a space where you don't need to be strong because everyone is going through the same thing. All of them own companies with similar characteristics, size, number of employees and revenue. So they all have similar problems. It's more effective than an MBA; the MBA gives you knowledge and good contacts, but a Mastermind group provides a sense of belonging to a very exclusive group of people.

Dan: It seems like an owners club.

Rony: I like the way you put it. The last Friday of this month I can invite you to a Mastermind I lead. It will be at the Fort Oak Restaurant at 2 p.m. If you want to be part of it, I need you to tell me no later than tomorrow and send me a signed NDA.

Dan: I'll sign it right now. It sounds interesting and mysterious.

Rony: You'll see how great things can come out. Above all it's a support group and it will make you accountable for your commitments.

Dan: It seems the same as an advisory board.

Rony: It seems to be, but they are two different things. Mastermind is for your personal and work-related development. An advisory board is to ensure the results of the organization. I have to go, but I'll meet you at the Mastermind meeting.

Conclusions:

❿ Having the right environment promotes better results. Business leaders feel lonely, but there's a lot of support around them. They only have to find it or create it.

 BUSINESS CONTINUITY.

> ❯ If you get run over by a truck, does your company survive?
>
> ❯ Anticipating different fatalistic scenarios helps in being prepared for eventualities and ensures continuity.

Rony: Hello Dan, let's talk about something that can be really uncomfortable and seems fatalistic, but it isn't.

Dan: You're scaring me Rony. You're always optimistic and cheerful. This sounds bad.

Rony: And I haven't explained it to you yet. It might get worse. Let's start. In the hypothetical case of a truck running over you, will your company survive? What will happen to all the work you have done? How can you ensure the wellbeing and heritage of your family?

Dan: So it really is a difficult subject. I hate talking about death.

Rony: Yes, me too. But it's something we have to talk about because, in theory, we're transforming your self-employment into a business, which should last with or without you. We talked about it the first time we met. This is one of the scenarios that can happen and possibly the most useful scenario for making crucial decisions.

Dan: Answering your previous question, no, the company wouldn't survive. There are many things depending on me right now. I'm the only one who has access to bank accounts.

Rony: So all those years of hard work could disappear? What will happen to your wife and kids?

Dan: I suppose Andrea would have to take my place and continue operating the company.

Rony: Is she prepared? Does she know anything about the company? Does she like it? Is she interested in it?

Dan: I don't think so, but we can train her.

Rony: Training Andrea is an option, but there are many others. Whoever you decide, has to be trained in advance. We should make a "recipe" to ensure the continuity of your company and the income of your family, better known as the Business Continuity Plan.

Dan: Seems like we're preparing my will.

Rony: You could say that. This document has to be prepared in advance with a plan of what to do in case something "bad" happens. Because not could only your absence destroy the company, but also other things like the 2008 financial crisis, a pandemic like covid-19 in 2020, a war, changes in law, etc. There are many scenarios and we can't prevent all of them, but if we are prepared for most of them, we can leave everything ready in case of an eventuality. Nowadays, almost every aspect of the company's operation is vulnerable to an interruption. The risk and cost of that interruption goes beyond information technologies. The **Business Continuity Management (BCM)** can be defined also with a compilation of processes that allow identifying and evaluating potential risks that could interrupt the regular activity of the organization. It helps to propose the right measures to take to reduce business impacts that the identified and evaluated risks could have on the company. Implementing BCM correctly can help you achieve the following objectives: guarantee the operational continuity of the company, establish priorities, and adjust prevention mechanisms, supervision and recovery before fault or disaster.

BCM has the following components:

1. **Business Impact Analysis (BIA)**
   a. Establish accident scenarios where the activity gets affected.
   b. Proceed to identify the affected systems.
   c. Quantify the economic impact.

2. **Disaster Recovery Plan (DRP)**

   a. A structured plan that allows the information recovery of the company systems.

   b. Establish procedures to back up the operation and support accident recovery.

3. **Business Continuity Plan (BCP)**

   a. It's the definition of accurate procedures to guarantee the continuity of operations.

   b. It ensures a backup of the information and the resources for the continuity of the operation.

Rony: In your case, you don't have partners, but when I work with someone who does, they should establish what happens with the wives and kids of each one of the partners if one of them dies. Some people choose that their families won't work at the company but will get paid with a salary, and also be paid company dividends. In other cases, the partner who stays alive has to buy the corresponding part of the other partner and pay the corresponding amount to the wife.

Dan: Oh, it sounds like a very delicate and uncomfortable issue, but I understand the need of being prepared to "survive bad situations".

Rony: A few years ago, I met a widowed lady who told me that when her husband died, she took care of his candy factory, which was very successful for 20 years. It took her four years to destroy what her husband built in 20. The factory disappeared along with the heritage of the family. She didn't know how to handle the company, and that's why it is very important to have a contingency plan, or in this case, a **succession plan.** We also need to have succession plans for your employees, because they aren't exempt from something happening to them, such as deciding to go to another company or greater situations; or something as simple as wanting a promotion or a different position.

Dan: Yes, that happens a lot. They leave the company and we all have to rush around looking for someone to replace them. But I don't see that happening if they want a promotion or a different position.

Rony: In 2016 I had a very interesting conversation with one of my mentors, Jim Tenuto, who lives in San Diego. He explained it with one phrase his philosophy about this issue: "If you are not replaceable, you are not promotable." I asked him to explain it to me in more detail, so he said that if someone at a company doesn't have someone else to replace them, they can't be promoted. This situation removes a lot of people's internal fears. People tend to fear developing their staff because we misguidedly think they can become our competition or that if there are people ready for my position that work below me, the boss can fire me. But the right focus should be: if I train my staff, I will have a better team, better results, and when the time's right, I could move to a different position because someone will be ready to replace me.

Dan: I think there's a TV series on HBO that talks about that, it's called "Succession".

Rony: Yes, there is. It's a very interesting series that represents how the leader of a very important company wants to prepare it for his absence, which actually happens. He has a disease and there's war between his children to see who would be the successor. I'm not telling you more because you should watch it, it'll give you some ideas.

Dan: Ok, I'll watch it.

Rony: It is very common that CEOs who are also founders feel trapped or even kidnapped by their employees, above all from those who are their right-hand men.

Dan: That's exactly how I feel with Victor. He became my right-hand man when the company was going through a critical moment. and I delegated all my operational responsibilities to him. At the beginning he was extraordinary, he helped me a lot; nevertheless, today he has become a monster. He dominates the operation, he won't let me see what's happening, his results aren't good, and on top of that, he's got me by the balls because he has threatened to leave the company, so I feel like I'm walking on eggshells and can't do anything about it because no one can handle his responsibilities. I depend entirely on him.

Rony: Has he openly threatened you with leaving? Or are you just assuming?

Dan: I assume. The truth is he has never openly said it, but I have the feeling and I have fear because many things depend on him, and to be honest, I don't want to move backwards.

Rony: That's a very uncomfortable situation because you can't demand results. It's a catch 22. A catch 22 trap is when someone gets affected by a situation in which any alternative he chooses is going to harm him. The term (catch 22) comes from the Catch 22 Joseph Heller novel, published in 1961. He narrates the story of an American pilot in WWII who tries to avoid conflict by impersonating a crazy person. Ironically, article 22 of the regulation establishes that no one in their sound judgment would want to pilot a bombing mission in such circumstances, so his allegation demonstrates he's really not crazy, and that he should continue flying the plane. According to this rule, every pilot who wants to fly demonstrates he's not in his right mind and must be replaced, but he has to send a review request. In that moment, the trap shuts down and the aviator is considered as sane because no mad man would present a complaint. There's no way of leaving the system. These kinds of logic traps are more frequent than we think, especially when referring to bureaucratic processes. In *Straight Dope* they present the example of an Australian citizen that moves to the USA and wants to insure his car. The insurance company asks him to demonstrate he is insurable, which implies he has to be previously insured in the USA; in the end, they don't grant him the insurance because he has no previous insurance. Something similar happens with immigrants, who are asked for a work visa before they can have a job, but they need a job so they can get the job permit.

Dan: That happens when people start looking for their first job. they are asked for work experience, which they obviously don't have, in order to have experience you need. But yes, definitely I feel in a Catch 22 with Victor. I can't demand anything from him because I fear he might leave, and that doesn't improve the efficiency of the operation. I feel trapped, frustrated and with no control.

Rony: And who created that situation?

Dan: He did.

Rony: Wrong. You did. You gave him that power. But everything is on your mind, you are the one who should feel in control. You have to control the fear of him leaving. You're describing a toxic situation, which is fed by fears and suppositions.

Dan: You're right. I've never seen it that way. My fear is what's imprisoning me, even though it's real.

Rony: Did you know "fear" is an acronym of False Evidence Appearing Real? Many fears we have aren't real. Being afraid activates a part of the brain which is called the amygdala, which controls emotions. It hasn't evolved a lot in our evolution as humans, so in some way it still operates as it did when we were cavemen. We had to be alert in case a wild animal attacked us and we had to either freeze, flee or fight; these are the three main reactions to fear. Today, most of us don't live with wild animals, we live in a peaceful environment. Nevertheless, the amygdala still operates similarly. People who work in marketing or in a news channel know this. They sell themselves through fear. Fear is naturally irrational, so it leads us to make irrational decisions.

Dan: That's the reason why I don't watch the news anymore, it makes me anxious.

Rony: Going back to Victor's situation. How many people are there in the market that could do things better than him? And even for less money?

Dan: I suppose many.

Rony: If you had candidates or replacements that could take Victor's position, do you think you'd also have fear?

Dan: Not at all. If I knew there were people available to start working immediately, I wouldn't feel threatened. Moreover, at Victor's first threat of quitting I would put him in his place and in case he leaves, I would hire his replacement right away.

Rony: That's the source of your fear, as you don't have a Virtual bench of candidates for the company. You're at your employee's mercy.

Dan: What's Virtual bench?

Rony: Virtual bench is a group of talent you've cultivated over time and that you can use whenever you need, according to the needs of the

company. It has to be cultivated and developed in advance, when you don't need it urgently. You have to keep an eye out to find excellent people that could add value and fill a position in your company. You can either search constantly for people to have on your virtual bench or just meet people at events, congress, summits, expositions, meetings, training, or even at Starbucks. You're always in contact with different people and anyone can be the right candidate.

Dan: Somehow it's like soccer, certain players of a First Division team are on the bench waiting to play in case they're needed, even when they have the same level of training as those who are on the field. How can I achieve that?

Rony: It's a practice and a habit. You always have to keep an eye out for who can be a candidate. The same way you follow up prospects to whom you can sell in a pipeline system with CRM like Zoho, you can have a list of possible candidates according to the positions of the company. You have to be in touch with them and recruit them over time to develop a good relationship. While the relationship is being built, you discover more about them, share the plan of scaling your company and how they can fit into it. You have to ensure the continuity of your company with the least anxiety possible. This is a very useful tool.

Dan: But today I don't have people on the Virtual bench to replace Victor or any other member of my team.

Rony: Well then, it's time to start searching for talent to replace any member of your team, including you.

Dan: Me? I don't want to leave the company.

Rony: I know you don't, but if something happens to you, the company would be at a high risk. That's why you can never be absent. It's a fatalistic way of thinking, but no one is exempt from having an accident. And on the optimistic side, there's the option of finding new and better business opportunities that require your attention.

Dan: That's true, I can't leave my family unprotected. I've invested so many years in shaping a patrimony to take care of my family in case I'm not here.

Rony: On the bright side, the fact that you have candidates to replace you is an opportunity to be free from the tasks that you're not very good at. There are people in the market that can do what you do in a more efficient and economical way, which gives you the possibility of doing the activities you really enjoy, and that adds more value.

Dan: In some way it's what I did with administration, a task that I hate. It distracts me from what's important, bores me, and I don't know much about it. I would love to focus on developing new products and making greater deals. But honestly, I don't have time for those activities because I'm immersed in the daily operation solving urgent, legal, and administrative matters. The members of the leading team have helped me take part of the burden and responsibility, but I don't feel like I'm ready for someone to take my place yet.

Rony: From my perspective, I don't think any of them are ready to be your replacement right now. But you have the option of developing one of them to replace you or even someone from outside the company. The idea is that the company grows to the point where you don't know how to handle it because of how much it grew, and that you can assume a stakeholder role. At that moment, you will have succeeded to level up and maintain the growth of the company.

Dan: Is it common that the founder stops being CEO but keeps working in a different area of the company like business development while reporting to the new CEO?

Rony: Only those founders who can control their egos achieve that. They ensure the continuity of the company, they focus on what they like and on what they're good at, they become stakeholders. If they don't take such a step, it's impossible for the company to evolve.

Dan: I don't know if my company would end up in my kids' hands many years from now, but definitely it would be helpful to start taking action so the company becomes more solid and ensures continuity.

Rony: In any of the following cases: employee loss, supplier bankruptcy, law restrictions, system changes, etc., you have to create a step-by-step plan along with your team so that they know how to

react. It's much easier to proceed once you have established protocols in case of an emergency, rather than making up the steps at the moment of the emergency. A perfect example of this is the aviation industry. every single time a plane is about to take off the crew repeats the security measures and in front of each passenger's seat there's a simple explanation of the steps to follow in case of an emergency. There's a QRH binder at the pilot's cabin with the specific steps they should follow in case of an accident. It's a very complete binder. In the movie *Sully*, based on the accident that occurred on the Hudson river, starring Tom Hanks, there's a scene where the pilot of the aircraft tells his copilot they just lost two of their engines, and that he should look at the QRH. This is something they don't explain in the movie and that most people don't know: QRH means Quick Reference Handbook. It's the manual with quick recommendations or a list of verified procedures for possible technical problems, abnormal situations and also emergency situations aboard the aircraft. It's not a flying manual or a manual of airplane operations. QRH is a format that's easy to use with the procedures mentioned before.

Dan: It's like a guide in case of emergency.

Rony: Yes, also for abnormal cases, alerts and failures. Pilots don't only have the binder at the cabin, but also several training sessions in simulators with different scenarios where they need to use the QRH. It's something they do to be prepared in advance in case of an emergency instead of having to react at the time of the emergency, which is much harder because of the anxiety and adrenaline they could feel at the moment.

Dan: At my elementary school there was an evacuation drill once a month. Whenever the alarm went off, we formed a line at the door and a few minutes later a boy in high school came to escort us. We practiced this continuously with the goal of doing it in less time. When I was in high school I was in charge of a group in elementary school. I had to be ready and to know different protocols in case of fire, bomb threat, earthquake or others. I remember there was a binder with different scenarios and the steps to follow. We had to know the steps by heart.

Thank god I never had to do any of the emergencies described in the binders.

Rony: Gather a work team of different areas and levels of the company to do the Business Continuity Plan exercise. They have to brainstorm possible fatalistic scenarios but without drifting to crazy ideas like an alien invasion or a meteorite hitting earth, realistic scenarios that can actually happen. After that, select the most realistic ideas, level of impact and level of risk for the company; that will give you the pattern to decide with which scenario you want to start working. You have to create a detailed response plan for each risk situation, with people in charge and their contact details. Once you have it ready, you have to test it by simulating those scenarios so you know whether they work. Then you can polish the analysis and the steps to follow. This information will be in a binder, and each director of the company should have access to it. Summing up, the steps are: identify and organize the threats; analyze the impact on the company; create a Business continuity plan, test the plan, and polish the analysis.

Dan: I suppose the Pentagon and armies around the world are specialized in doing these exercises to know how to react to different scenarios.

Rony: Exactly. Those teams prepare the most for those scenarios. If they do it and practice it continuously, I don't see why companies shouldn't do it too. In September 2017 thousands of Mexican companies suffered physical, health and financial damages for not being prepared for a strong earthquake and not knowing which actions to take automatically, so in the face of an immediate crisis their decisions were emotional, and on many occasions, not efficient. In my case, I was just starting to work with a customer who has a call center. His company was affected by the earthquake. I gathered with his leading team so they could make emergency decisions, but we couldn't enter the building or access the servers. If he had had his BCP ready, he could have had an action protocol ready for an earthquake. In Mexico these types of phenomena are frequent; in 1985 the city was also devastated. If people used that experience, the reaction of the team would have

been proactive, controlled and systematic, but instead it was reactive, chaotic and unpredictable.

Dan: I definitely want a proactive, controlled and systematic company. I would rather spend some time thinking and more time acting. As Thomas Alva Edison said, "1% inspiration and 99% perspiration." I will make the time to do this exercise with the team, and to make the BCP binder, at least with basic scenarios.

Rony: For this process you can include the Mastermind people and your advisory board, so they can help you have a more complete vision and plan. Many of your Mastermind colleagues already have a plan because they already went through the uncomfortable process of doing an exercise like this.

Conclusions:

❯ To ensure the continuity of your company is more than a desire, it's making plans and taking a directed action so your company can be more prepared and shielded from eventualities.

 16 CONCLUSIONS.

> **❱** "We are products of our past, but we don't have to be prisoners of it." Rick Warren.
>
> **❱** "It's only after you've stepped outside your comfort zone that you begin to change, grow, and transform." Roy T. Bennet.

The growth of a company isn't a game of chance, it's a process with a methodology behind it. Any owner of a fast-growing company can implement the diverse tools described in this book to organize and regain the growth of the company.

The CEO/founder shouldn't be at the mercy of the company's needs or feel trapped in a vicious cycle which he created through time and makes him feel like everything depends on him alone, trapped and frustrated. On the contrary, business should be something that the CEO enjoys, controls, and makes good use of. Businesses are tools for achieving personal goals and contributing to society.

We started this book talking about the complexity of growing a company and about how some decisions, with time, can make daily operations difficult, not to mention a growth plan. We have to understand the stage where the company is and apply the tools needed accordingly.

In the story of Dan, Plastypack's CEO, we had a journey through organizational change and development, the series of tools that were implemented are used by medium-sized and fast growth companies around the world. There's no precise formula with a specific order to implement these tools because each company has different needs according to the

moment they're living in; nevertheless, all the tools that were described are useful and must be applied to regain control of the company, so probably the order presented is the most accurate.

Even though this story was based on a company that sells products, these principles also apply to companies that provide services, because the problems that are presented in the process of organizational change and growth are the same.

This process can last from 12 to 18 months. There's no need to make all of the adjustments at the same time. You must apply one tool at a time, evaluate results and make the pertinent adjustments. There are companies that can implement more tools in less time, but this isn't a 100-meter race, it's a marathon for which you have to be patient, hang in there and be persistent.

Enter our web pages https://adaptable.com.mx/contenidos-eventos/herramientas/ and http://www.colanomuevaalperro.com/, where you'll find tools, formats, meeting agendas and more, which you can download for free, so you can start implementing the changes that you need.

We joined Dan, Plastypack's CEO, through his journey of organizational change and development. We started identifying his organizational GPS, understanding his current situation or point A, as clearly as possible to understand the reality of the company and some of the main causes of his actual complexity.

Then, we established a vision, the second part of the GPS or point B, the final destination where the entrepreneur wants to go with as much clarity as possible, focusing his efforts towards that destination.

Afterwards, we identified the particular language with which the company has to develop its "organizational dictionary" in order to reduce confusion and rework.

We learned the different stages of the organization, the most common problems and toxic habits, according to the moment the company is living in, which depends mainly on the number of people and the revenue the company has.

Later, we incorporated the leadership team to the process, which would support the CEO directly not only by implementing the tools, but also properly handling daily tasks, which releases the CEO's potential and also that of each leader in their department, which smooths decision making.

We also integrated more people to the issue, so they can own the solutions, which usually are very creative because those are the people who live with these issues day to day. We generated the right organizational structure based on the needs and reality of the company.

We explored different ways to make decisions, which had to be shared at the meetings to have clear expectations and be able to make appropriate decisions. Further on, we created different dashboards and KPIs that visually reflect the reality of the company, in order to stop working under suppositions and urges;, to focus on proactivity, into what actually matters.

Once you can measure individual, group and organizational performance, a culture of accountability, where people's commitments start to weigh more, they start to think that they should either meet their commitments or stop making them, which creates reliability.

Then, we explored work meetings as a tool that should be used correctly to allow maintaining the syncing of the members and generate the right progress towards the desired goals.

We continued with the core business definition, which helps identify the main solutions that the company can build for its customers and at the same time eliminates distractions, which allows the company to be more effective and selective.

Once we had that clear, we were able to deeply understand the different products that the company has and pledged for those that really contribute to its success, becoming extraordinary in a few things instead of mediocre in many with the help of Pareto's principle (80/20) and the ABC matrix of products.

Thanks to this analysis, we understood who the customers are to whom we can really provide an extraordinary service. We identified "Top 10" customers and learned that the company has to focus its actions on satisfying the needs of this exclusive group.

We understood the employee's life cycle in the organization, from attraction to separation, and we mentioned a series of strategies that improves the company's reputation, which will make the job of Human Resources easier. We also learned about the employee categorization according to the Talent Map, where we evaluated attitude vs. aptitude together.

We moved forward with the evaluation of suppliers, who are the commercial partners of the company, and identified those who will support the growth of the company and the actions to take to ensure having an effective operation.

Later on, we explored several elements of the environment that promote the changes at the company, such as order, discipline, organization, cleanliness, Mastermind groups, coaching support and external consultants.

All those subjects consolidated with the last point of the continuity of the company, for the purpose of ensuring that the company survives different situations that could happen, including the death of the CEO. Thus, the heritage that was built with so much effort can be protected and shielded.

Now that you've finished this book and understand some of the different tools that you can use, it's time for you to put them to practice.

At the beginning, it will be a little complicated, but with time you'll see how the pieces of the puzzle start to fit and the image will be clearer.

It's not about implementing all the tools at once, but one tool at a time while measuring the progress of the organization, so you can find a way to take control of your company.

# 17 REFERENCES.

Websites

http://www.npscalculator.com/en

https://hbr.org/2009/05/why-teams-dont-work

https://www.statista.com/statistics/795813/hours-of-training-per-employee-by-company-size-us/)

https://www.youtube.com/watch?v=KkAlRZ8F4LI

Bibliography

Adizes, I. (1988). *Corporate lifecycles: how and why corporations grow and die and what to do about it.* Englewood Cliffs, N. J.: Prentice Hall.

Bloom, R. H. and Conti, D. (2008). *The inside advantage: the strategy that unlocks the hidden growth in your business.* New York: McGraw-Hill.

Bossidy, L., Charan, R. and Burck, Ch. (2002). *Execution: the discipline of getting things done.* New York: Crown Business.

Bustin, G. (2014). *Accountability: the key to driving a high-performance culture.* New York: McGraw-Hill Education.

Collins, J. C. and Hansen, M. T. (2011). *Great by choice: uncertainty, chaos, and luck: why some thrive despite them all.* New York, NY: HarperCollins Publishers.

Collins, J. C. and Porras, J. (1995). *Built to last: successful habits of visionary companies.* London: Century Business.

Collins, J. C. and Hansen, M. T. (2011). *Great by choice: uncertainty, chaos, and luck: why some thrive despite them all.* New York, NY: HarperCollins Publishers.

Coyle, D. (2018). *The culture code: the secrets of highly successful groups.* New York: Bantam Books.

Crabtree, G. and Harzog, B. (2011). *Simple numbers, straight talk, big profits!: 4 keys to unlock your business potential.* Austin, Tex: Greenleaf Book Group Press.

De Boer, L., Labro, E. and Morlacchi, P. A (2001). Review of methods supporting supplier selection. *European Journal of Purchasing and Supply Management.*

Dickson, G. (1966). An analysis of vendor selection systems and decisions. *Journal of Purchasing & Supply Management.*

Drucker, P. F. (1993). *Managing for results: economic tasks and risk-taking decisions.* New York: Harper Business.

Goffin, K. and Lemke, F. (2006). An exploratory study of "close" supplier–manufacturer relationships. *Journal of Operations Management.*

Goldratt, E. M. and Cox, J. (2004). *The goal: a process of ongoing improvement.* Aldershot: Gower.

Hamel, G. and Prahalad, C. K. (1994). *Competing for the future.* Boston, Mass: Harvard Business School Press.

Harnish, Verne. Mastering Rockefeller habits. Ashburn, Virginia.

Harnish, V. (2014). *Scaling up.* Ashburn, Virginia: Gazelles Inc.

Herold, C. (2011). *DOUBLE DOUBLE: How to Double Your Revenue and Profit in 3 Years or Less.* Austin, Texas: GREENLEAF Book Group Press.

Hoffman, J. and Finkel, D. (2014). *Scale: seven proven principles to grow your business and get your life back.* New York: Portfolio Hardcover.

Huang, S. and Keskar, H. (2007). Comprehensive and configurable metrics for supplier selection. *International Journal of Production Economics.*

Ismail, S. *et al.* (2014). *Exponential organizations: why new organizations are ten times better, faster, and cheaper than yours (and what to do about it).* New York, New York: Diversion Books.

Kim, W C. and Mauborgne, R. (2005). *Blue ocean strategy: how to create uncontested market space and make the competition irrelevant.* Boston, Mass: Harvard Business School Press.

LeBlanc, L. A., Nosik, M. R. Planning and Leading Effective Meetings. *Behav. Analysis Practice* 12, 696-708 (2019). https://doi.org/10.1007/s40617-019-00330-z

Lencioni, P. (2003). Five dysfunctions of a Team.

Logan, D., King, J. and Wright, H. (2011). *Tribal leadership: leveraging natural groups to build a thriving organization*. New York: Harper Business.

Michalowicz, M. (2012). *The pumpkin plan: a simple strategy to grow a remarkable business in any field*. New York: Portfolio/Penguin.

Moran, R. A. (2011). *Sins and CEOs: lessons from leaders and losers that will change your career*. New York: Heliotrope Books.

Osterwalder, A. *et al.* (2014). *Value proposition design: how to create products and services customers want*. Hoboken: John Wiley & Sons.

Praes, J. (2005). *Esquezofrenia: manual para una nueva vida*. México: Jacobo Neuman Praes.

Priestley, D. (2017). *24 assets: create a digital, scalable, valuable and fun business that will thrive in a fast changing world*. Gorleston Great Britain: Dent. Books.

Reichheld, F. F. and Markey, R. (2011). *The ultimate question 2.0: how net promoter companies thrive in a customer-driven world*. Boston, Mass: Harvard Business Press.

Tilson, B. R. (2018). *Go slow to grow fast: how to keep your company driving and thriving in a fast-paced, competitive business world*. Charleston, South Carolina: ForbesBooks.

Voss, C. and Raz, T. (2017). *Never split the difference: negotiating as if your life depended on it*. London: Rh Business Books.

Wickman, G. (2011). *Traction: get a grip on your business*. Dallas, TX: BenBella Books.

Shirkani, J. (2013). *Ego vs. EQ: how top leaders beat 8 ego traps with emotional intelligence*. Brookline, MA: Bibliomotion, Inc.

Zook, C. and Allen, J. (2016). *The founder's mentality: how to overcome the predictable crises of growth*. Boston, Massachusetts: Harvard Business Review Press.

MW01615953